Environmental Print Activities

Karen L. Bauer, EdD

Maureen Walcavich, EdD

LeAnne Nipps, BS

Carson-Dellosa Publishing Company, Inc.

Greensboro, North Carolina

Credits

Editor
Joey Bland

Layout Design
Van Harris

Inside Illustrations
Van Harris
Lori Jackson

Cover Design
Matthew Van Zomeren

                                    ISBN 1-59441-485-8

Table of Contents

Overview

What Is Environmental Print?

Environmental print is the print we see all around us. It is the print on everyday products we use, on street signs, and on logos. It is the print we recognize because of its shape, pictures, and colors. Honey Nut Cheerios® and Lucky Charms® cereal boxes/logos, stop signs and railroad crossing signs, and McDonald's® and Burger King® logos are all examples of environmental print.

Although valuable, labels on shelves in the classroom, word cards identifying the door, window, or CD player, and children's names written on crayon boxes, cubbies, or pictures, do not constitute environmental print. Rather, these are examples of words found in a print-rich environment. Most early childhood teachers display print at each center in their rooms and label supplies and objects. Teachers may often neglect to capitalize on what children already know and experience in their world every day. They fail to incorporate environmental print in the curriculum and the classroom.

Why Use Environmental Print?

Environmental print surrounds children. This print is "embedded" in their world. Children begin their literacy learning as they observe environmental print and construct an understanding of its meaning in context (Harste, Burke, and Woodward, 1982). When children go to fast food restaurants, they get much more than a burger and fries. "They are increasingly able to construct meaning from their expanding world as they encounter symbols, signs, labels, and logos" (West and Egley, 1998).

"Informal, everyday experiences with print in their lives appear to be a crucial part of children's literacy learning process" (Morrow, Strickland, and Woo, 1998). Using environmental print with children is a good choice because it is the first type of print children recognize and understand as their literacy skills begin to emerge. Children begin to recognize environmental print at a young age. By the age of three, children recognize the logos of fast food chains. By age four, children can identify products, logos, labels, and signs. Four- and five-year-olds begin copying words found on media, signs, and logos.

Environmental print offers children opportunities to understand their world and the ways in which adults use literacy in meaningful contexts. Environmental print surrounds children and provides meaningful literacy experiences with reading material that is familiar to them. As a result, children feel successful reading environmental print. Success is motivating. Children begin to see themselves as readers and writers and want to read and write more.

Environmental print can be integrated into any curriculum area. The use of environmental print throughout the curriculum helps make learning meaningful. Classification and graphing activities using environmental print support mathematical thinking. Sorting foods into healthy and unhealthy choices or into food groups

provides science content. A unit on the community can incorporate learning about traffic signs and safety, identifying local business and recreation sites, learning the names of streets, and constructing maps of the area.

Environmental print is readily available and inexpensive. Teachers and parents can collect environmental print easily and regularly. Having a supply of environmental print allows teachers to provide numerous and varied experiences for children.

Environmental print is, therefore, a logical place to begin when planning literacy experiences. Teachers of young children can prepare an assortment of activities with environmental print and incorporate these activities into various centers and with a variety of themes to expand children's emerging literacy. Environmental print can be used as a building block for developing young children's literacy skills. Incidental experiences, however, are insufficient. Planned, sequential experiences with environmental print that build children's understanding of reading and writing are critical.

The Environmental Print Learning Continuum

Teachers need a framework from which they can plan sequential experiences to facilitate children's understanding of reading and writing. The Environmental Print Learning Continuum (see page 6) offers teachers such a framework. This 10-step hierarchy identifies increasingly complex literacy skills that teachers of preschool children can develop through planned, sequential experiences with environmental print. By providing experiences with environmental print at each step of the continuum, teachers enhance and expand young children's understanding of reading and writing.

The Environmental Print Learning Continuum also provides a way for teachers to assess and evaluate young children's literacy skills using appropriate activities. It is important to view assessment and evaluation as an integral component of the instructional process. Monitoring children's developing literacy skills provides teachers with valuable information to plan future experiences. An easy way for teachers to monitor children's growth and progress with environmental print is to use a checklist. A checklist is a collection of learning objectives that match the developmental sequence of a hierarchy of skills. As children engage in various activities designed to promote development of skills on the continuum, teachers can observe and record children's progress on a checklist. Checklists completed for individual children can be placed in a child's portfolio and shared with parents during conferences (page 94). Checklists can also be completed for the entire class (page 95). This information can be used to help teachers form flexible groups for instruction. For example, children whose skills are more advanced might be paired to participate in an activity with children who are just beginning to develop a skill.

By using active, appropriate activities at each step of the continuum, assessment and evaluation can be an integral, ongoing process which provides guidance for teachers to plan increasingly more complex experiences for each child.

Environmental Print Learning Continuum

1   **Point to Environmental Print**

2   **Match Environmental Print**

3   **Identify Environmental Print**

4   **Name Individual Letters**

5   **Copy Print**

6   **Match Decontextualized Words**

7   **Classify by Category**

8   **Dictate Stories**

9   **Classify by Initial Sounds**

10   **Classify by Syllables**

Using the Environmental Print Learning Continuum

The Environmental Print Learning Continuum identifies increasingly complex literacy skills. Preschool children's abilities to work with environmental print will correspond to various points on the continuum. Teachers must identify those skills children already possess and plan experiences to facilitate their progress along the continuum. Large- and small-group activities that involve children working individually, in pairs, or with the teacher one-on-one are all possible.

The easiest skill on the continuum, **pointing to environmental print**, involves a child's ability to point to specific pieces of environmental print identified by the teacher.

The second skill on the environmental print continuum involves the child's ability to **match environmental print**. Children who have acquired this skill are able to match identical environmental print although they may not yet be able to read the print.

Identifying environmental print is the third skill on the continuum. At this stage, children can read a sample of environmental print without assistance.

Naming individual letters is more difficult than identifying specific environmental print and is the next skill on the continuum. Because recognizing the letters in their names is highly meaningful for children, teachers can begin to teach this skill by providing opportunities for children to find the letters in their names in environmental print.

Opportunities for experimenting with making letters and words should be a major part of the literacy curriculum because children's reading and writing skills develop simultaneously. **Copying print** is the fifth skill on the environmental print continuum. Initially, teachers can provide experiences with environmental print that allow children to trace over letters. As children advance, they can copy environmental print onto paper, chalkboards, and white boards.

Children will gradually acquire the ability to read decontextualized words in books on their own (Tompkins, 2003). Teachers can, however, use environmental print to help children **match decontextualized print** with contextualized print as a precursor to reading decontextualized words in books. Often, when print is separated from its familiar environmental context, young children have difficulty identifying it. They may not realize that McDonald's® is the same thing as the "golden arches." It is necessary that children understand that a word is made of a group of letters that can be read. It is important to provide young children with many opportunities to match decontextualized words with the words in context.

Sorting objects by common attributes is an acquired skill that is a prerequisite for reading, spelling, and decoding words. To develop this ability, children should have opportunities to sort and classify items. After children have had experiences sorting actual objects, they can **classify environmental print** by category. Environmental print can be classified in many ways. Environmental print exists for food items, street and traffic signs, restaurants, toys, and stores. Children can begin by creating broad classifications such as food or nonfood items and gradually create more refined classifications.

The next skill on the Environmental Print Learning Continuum is **dictating stories**. Young children enjoy relating personal events and sharing them with others. Writing what children dictate and having them read their dictation contributes to children's ability to read. Children can be encouraged to select logos, labels, or other environmental print that they know and make up stories about them. When the dictation is transcribed, the environmental print logo or label should be included in the written product. A trip to Arby's® could be the focus of a story that a child dictates. The Arby's® logo would be included every time the word Arby's® is in the child's story. Then, the child and teacher read the written story together.

Experiences that provide children with opportunities to **classify environmental print by initial sound** will depend on the ages and abilities of the children. Children may be able to identify environmental print that starts with the same sounds as their names. Additional experiences will provide children with opportunities to expand their abilities to identify letter sounds.

Playing with sounds should be an extensive part of any literacy program. Chanting, rhyming, and clapping the number of sounds in words should be an integral part of children's literacy experiences in the classroom. Being able to **classify environmental print by syllables** requires children to have a variety of opportunities to play with the sounds in words. Using environmental print allows teachers to provide children with visual and auditory experiences in recognizing the number of syllables in words and classifying words by syllables.

The Environmental Print Learning Continuum provides a framework for teachers to plan increasingly complex literacy experiences for young children using environmental print. The goal of these experiences is to expand young children's literacy skills. The experiences teachers offer at each skill level of the Environmental Print Learning Continuum will depend on the ages and abilities of the children. Numerous and varied activities should be provided at each level of the Continuum. Assessment of children's abilities should be an integral, ongoing process as children progress in their experiences with environmental print using the Continuum.

This book provides numerous ways for teachers to use environmental print with young children. The organization of the ideas is based on the Environmental Print Learning Continuum. Teachers can begin using the activities that match their students' abilities and continue to develop students' literacy skills as they move through the continuum. To monitor children's literacy growth with environmental print, two checklists are provided on pages 94–95. Use the first checklist to record individual children's skills. Use the second checklist to track the entire class.

Level 1

Point to Environmental Print

Main Objective:

Children will be able to point to environmental print identified by the teacher.

Rationale:

Children develop an awareness of written language as a form of communication. They recognize that print has meaning. They begin to understand that specific print has specific meaning. For example, they understand that cereal boxes with Kix® on the fronts all contain the same type of cereal and that a McDonald's® sign indicates a specific type of fast-food restaurant. Knowledge that print has meaning is crucial to literacy development.

The activities in this section provide children with a variety of ways to respond to requests to point to environmental print identified by the teacher. The child may not be able to read the environmental print independently, but with the teacher's prompting will be able to point to the named print.

Puzzles

Objective:

Children will be able to point to the name of the cereal.

Materials and Construction:

- Two identical front panels from empty cereal boxes
- Scissors
- One 2-quart (1.89 L) resealable, plastic bag
- Clear contact paper or laminating film

Cut the front panels from two identical empty cereal boxes. Cut one front panel into puzzle pieces. The number of puzzle pieces will depend on the age of the children. Keep the second front panel intact to use as the model for the puzzle. Use clear contact paper or laminating film to cover the puzzle pieces and the model for the puzzle. Store the puzzle and model in a resealable, plastic bag.

Procedures:

Have a child take the puzzle pieces and the model of the puzzle out of the bag. Once the child has completed the puzzle, ask her to point to the words in the cereal's name.

Adaptations:

- Use the front panels of cracker or cookie boxes to make puzzles.
- Glue the labels from canned fruits or vegetables on card stock to make puzzles.

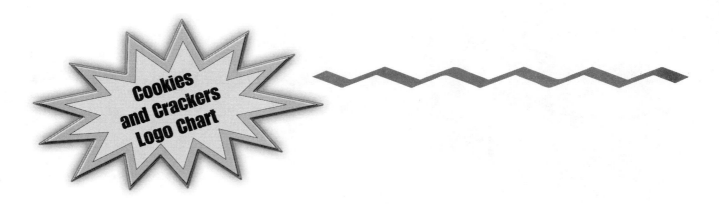

Cookies and Crackers Logo Chart

Objective:

Children will be able to point to the cookie or cracker identified by the teacher.

Materials and Construction:

- 24" x 36" (61 cm x 91 cm) sheet of poster board
- Labels/front panels from various types of cookie and cracker packages
- Scissors
- Glue stick
- Clear contact paper or laminating film

Cut the labels/front panels from various types of cookie and cracker packages. Glue the environmental print on the 24" x 36" (61 cm x 91 cm) sheet of poster board. Use six labels/front panels for three- or four-year-olds. Use more labels/front panels for older children. Cover the chart with clear contact paper or laminate for durability.

Procedures:

For this activity, you may work with an individual child, a small group, or the entire class. Have children sit facing the chart. After you name a cookie or cracker on the chart, have one child come to the chart and point to the product you identified.

Adaptations:

- Make duplicate labels/front panels of the cookie and cracker packages. Ask a child to select the duplicate label/front panel and match it to the same product on the chart.
- Mount pictures of cookies and crackers on the chart with hook-and-loop tape. Change the products as children become familiar with print.

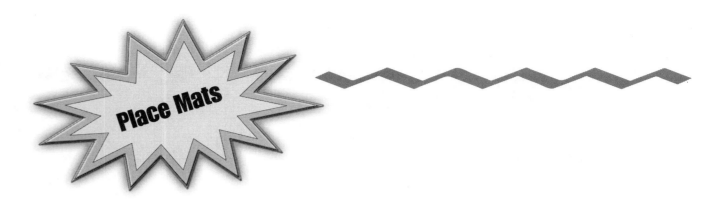

Objective:

Children will be able to point to the environmental print on the place mats when prompted.

Materials and Construction:

- 8.5" x 17" (21.6 cm x 43 cm) pieces of poster board (one for each child)
- Variety of environmental print cut from products such as crackers, candy bars, and drinks
- Glue sticks
- Scissors
- Clear contact paper or laminating film

Provide each child with a piece of 8.5" x 17" (21.6 cm x 43 cm) poster board. Make a variety of environmental print available for children to select. Have children glue different pieces of environmental print on the pieces of poster board to create their place mats. When the children are finished, cover the fronts and backs of the place mats with clear contact paper or laminating film.

Procedure:

Use the place mats at snack time and lunchtime. Ask children to find specific products on their place mats.

Adaptations:

- Cut out fast-food and restaurant logos from bags, napkins, etc., to create the place mats.
- Make seasonal or thematic place mats such as leaf-shaped place mats for fall or place mats with only logos of crackers.

Objective:

Children will be able to point to the environmental print named on the "house."

Materials and Construction:

- Large cardboard box from a washer, dryer, stove, or dishwasher
- Environmental print from cookie, candy, snack, and cereal packages (enough to cover the cardboard box)
- Scissors
- Glue sticks
- Craft knife

Using the craft knife, cut out windows and a door for the "Hansel and Gretel" house.

Procedures:

Read and discuss the story of "Hansel and Gretel" with children. Show them the large box on which you have already cut out the door and windows. Explain to the class that they will be making the witch's house from the story "Hansel and Gretel." Tell children to glue the environmental print on the box, making sure that the print does not overlap. Provide the children with glue sticks and the environmental print to create the house. Once the house is complete, reread the story and have the children act out the story. Ask children to find specific environmental print on the house. Place the book near the house and allow the children to retell the story and identify environmental print during free choice time.

Adaptations:

- Use shoe boxes to make individual "Hansel and Gretel" houses for each child.
- Cut out paper in the shapes of houses. Have children glue environmental print that they can read on their houses. Use the houses to create a mural.

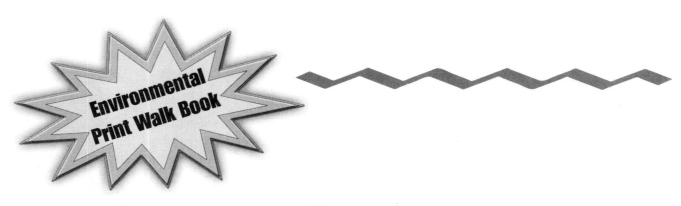

Objective:

Children will be able to find the environmental print in the Environmental Print Walk Book.

Materials and Construction:

- Camera with film or a digital camera
- Small photo album that holds one picture per page
- Unlined index card
- Marker

Take the children on an environmental print walk in the neighborhood around your school. Let them know that they need to look for environmental print (signs, logos, etc.). Take photos of street signs, traffic signs, neighborhood stores, etc. Place the photos in the small photo album. Make sure you have a title page for the album.

Procedures:

Gather children together on the floor in front of you. Discuss the environmental print walk and ask children to recall the different environmental print they saw on their walk. Display the Environmental Print Walk Book and read the title with the children. Show them individual pictures in the book and read the print on each page. Next, invite one child to find a specific piece of environmental print in the book. Repeat with several children. Place the book in your classroom library.

Adaptations:

- Make duplicate copies of the photos. Have children find the identical photo in the Environmental Print Walk Book.
- Use the duplicate prints to sequence the environmental print walk. Have children read the environmental print as they sequence the pictures.

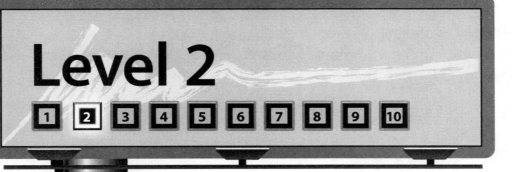

Level 2

Match Environmental Print

Main Objective:

Children will be able to match two identical pieces of environmental print.

Rationale:

Recognizing the shapes and names of letters is important to literacy. Experiences with matching environmental print provide children with opportunities to notice the shapes of letters and to discriminate among written symbols.

Level 2 activities involve the child's ability to match environmental print. Children who have acquired this skill are able to match identical environmental print although they may not be able to read the print.

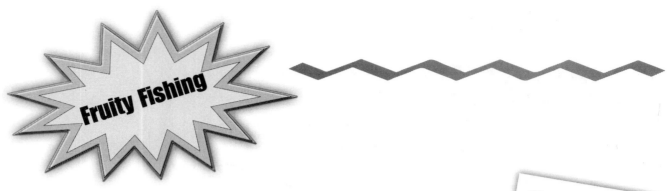

Objective:

Children will be able to match the two cards that are alike by playing the card game Go Fish.

Materials and Construction:

- 32 4" x 6" (10 cm x 15.24 cm) unlined index cards
- Four labels each from eight different canned fruits
- Die
- Glue stick
- Scissors
- Clear contact paper or laminating film
- Sandwich-size resealable, plastic bag

Cut the labels off of the cans of fruit and glue them on the 4" x 6" (10 cm x 15.24 cm) index cards. Make two identical sets of each picture. There will be four cards of each fruit (for example, four cards with peaches). The card deck will have a total of 32 cards. Cover the fronts and backs of the cards with clear contact paper or laminate for durability. Store the cards in the resealable bag.

Procedures:

Two to four children can play Fruity Fishing at one time. Have each player roll the die. The player with the highest number deals the cards. The dealer gives three cards to each player and places the remaining cards facedown on the table (the Go Fish pile). Play starts with the child to the right of the dealer (Player 1) who asks the player to his right (Player 2) for a card. (For example, "Do you have any peaches?") If Player 2 has the card, she gives it to Player 1, who places the matching card on the table and goes again. If Player 2 does not have the card Player 1 asked for, Player 2 says, "Go fish." Then, Player 1 takes the top card from the Go Fish pile. If Player 1 gets a match from the Go Fish pile, he lays down the matching cards and goes again. If there is no match, the next child takes a turn.

Adaptations:

- Make cards from other samples of environmental print.
- Lay all cards facedown in a circle on the table. Have a child pick up cards until he finds a match. Replace cards that do not match. Play then moves to the next child.

 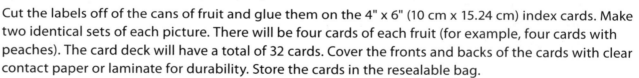

Vegetable Concentration

Objective:

Children will be able to match the two cards that are alike while playing concentration.

Materials and Construction:

- 4" x 6" (10 cm x 15.24 cm) unlined index cards
- Two identical labels from five to eight different canned vegetables
- Die
- Scissors
- Glue stick
- Clear contact paper or laminating film
- Sandwich-size resealable, plastic bag

Cut the labels off of the cans of vegetables. Glue the labels on the 4" x 6" (10 cm x 15.24 cm) unlined index cards using the glue stick. Cover both sides of the cards with clear contact paper or laminating film for durability. Store in the resealable, plastic bag.

Procedures:

Two to four children can play Vegetable Concentration at one time. Shuffle and place the cards facedown in rows on a table. Have each player roll the die. The player with the highest number goes first. She turns over two cards. If the cards match, the child keeps the cards, then takes another turn. If the cards do not match, the next child takes a turn. Encourage children to name the vegetables as they turn over the cards.

Adaptations:

- Use mini-cereal boxes to create concentration cards.
- Use candy bar wrappers to create concentration cards.

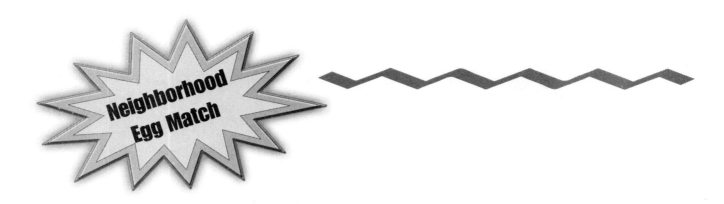

Objective:

Children will be able to match the two egg "halves" with the same environmental print.

Materials and Construction:

- Two copies each of 4" x 6" (10 cm x 15.24 cm) photos of community buildings, stores, and restaurants taken in the neighborhood surrounding your school
- Card stock to make paper eggs
- Scissors
- Glue stick
- Clear contact paper or laminating film
- One 2-quart (1.89 L) resealable, plastic bag

Take photos of the police station, fire station, stores, and restaurants in your school's neighborhood. Be sure to include the names of the buildings, stores, or restaurants in the photos since these are the environmental print for this activity. Make two copies of each 4" x 6" (10 cm x 15.24 cm) photo. Cut out egg shapes from the card stock. The egg shapes should be large enough to hold two photos. Glue identical building photos on an egg shape, one on each half, and cut the egg into two puzzle pieces. Cover the egg puzzle pieces with clear contact paper or laminating film. Store in the resealable, plastic bag. This is a good individual and group activity.

Procedures:

Have children take the egg puzzles out of the bags. They will assemble each puzzle by matching the identical environmental print on the two egg parts.

Adaptations:

- Use leaves, flowers, apples, or other seasonal shapes for the puzzle pieces.
- Create an interactive bulletin board with the puzzle pieces.

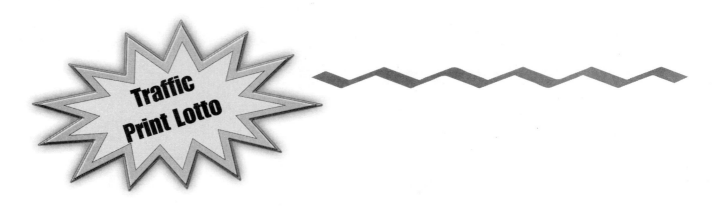

Objective:

Children will be able to match the traffic signs.

Materials and Construction:

- Computer
- Printer
- 8.5" x 11" (21.6 cm x 28 cm) printer paper
- Traffic signs printed from the Internet
- 8.5" x 11" (21.6 cm x 28 cm) card stock
- 3" x 3.5" (7.6 cm x 9 cm) pieces of card stock
- One 2-quart (1.89 L) resealable, plastic bag
- Die
- Ruler
- Marker
- Scissors
- Glue stick
- Clear contact paper or laminating film

To obtain traffic signs, go to an Internet search engine such as Google®, AltaVista™, etc. Click on Images, type "traffic signs" in the search window, and then click Search. Select 10–15 traffic signs from the images to use on the lotto cards. Print the selected traffic signs on the printer paper. To create the lotto cards, divide the 8.5" x 11" (21.6 cm x 28 cm) card stock into a 3 x 3 grid (nine rectangles in the grid approximately 3" x 3.5" (7.6 cm x 9 cm). Create six lotto cards. Glue nine images on each lotto card grid. Make individual traffic sign cards (approximately 3" x 3.5" or 7.6 cm x 9 cm) that match the traffic signs on the lotto cards. There will be a total of 54 individual traffic sign cards. Cover the lotto cards and individual traffic sign cards with clear contact paper or laminating film. Store in the resealable, plastic bag. (See illustration on page 20.)

Procedures:

Six children can play Traffic Print Lotto at one time. Have each child select a traffic sign lotto card. Shuffle the individual traffic sign cards and put them facedown in a pile. Let each child roll the die. The player with the highest number goes first. The first child draws a card and looks at the traffic sign. If that traffic sign is on the child's lotto card, the child places it over the picture. If the traffic sign is not on the child's lotto card, the individual traffic sign card goes on the bottom of the pile. Play then moves to the next child. The winner is the first player to have three signs covered in a row across, down, or diagonally. Encourage children to identify the traffic signs.

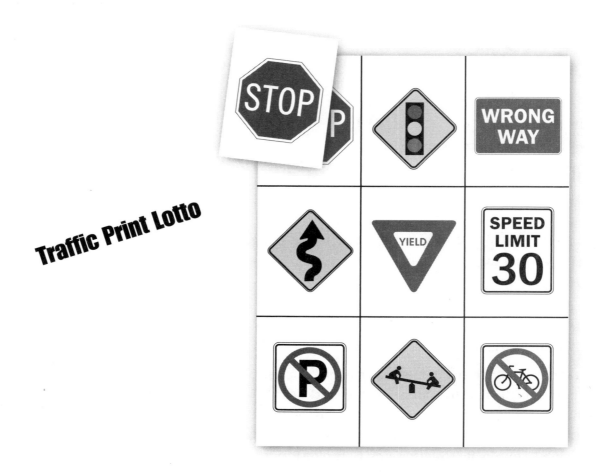

Traffic Print Lotto

Adaptations:

- Children must cover all of the signs on the card to win.
- Play as a bingo game instead of a lotto game. Give each child a traffic sign lotto card and nine bingo chips. Shuffle the individual traffic sign cards and put them in a pile. Show children the first traffic sign. If that traffic sign is on a child's card, he should cover it with a bingo chip. Play continues until one child has three signs covered in a row across, down, or diagonally.

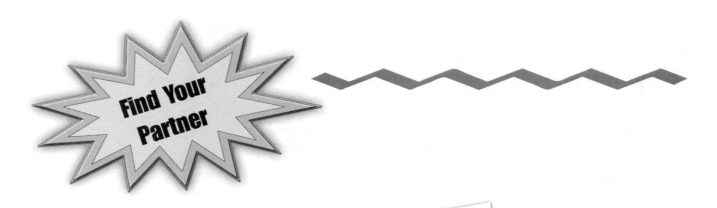

Find Your Partner

Objective:

Children will be able to find the partner who has the same environmental print sign.

Materials and Construction:

- Two copies each of various environmental print (for example, mini-cereal boxes or labels from canned products)
- 5" x 8" (12.7 cm x 20.3 cm) unlined index cards
- Glue stick
- Scissors
- Clear contact paper or laminating film

Collect two copies each of a variety of environmental print. Glue the print on card stock so that there are two cards for each piece of environmental print. Create enough cards to give one to each child. Cover the environmental print cards with clear contact paper or laminate for durability.

Procedures:

Give each child one environmental print card. Have children look at their cards and then hold the cards in front of them. The children must walk around and look at each card until they find the environmental print that matches their cards. After everyone has found his partner, help the children read the environmental print.

Adaptations:

- Have children stand opposite each other in two lines. Pass out one set of cards to the children in each line. One at a time, each child must walk to the other side and find her partner.
- Put half of the environmental print on sentence strips and half on index cards. Children can wear the sentence strips as headbands. The children with the cards must find partners wearing headbands with the same print that is on their cards.

Level 3
Identify Environmental Print

Main Objective:
Children will be able to read environmental print.

Rationale:
Children are usually able to recognize the print on products, signs, restaurant packaging, etc. Young emergent readers, however, depend on context to read familiar words. The shapes, pictures, and colors of environmental print help children to read the print. Children develop relationships linking the form and meaning of environmental print as they have continued experiences with such print.

Level 3 activities involve children's ability to read environmental print in context without assistance. These experiences expand children's opportunities to interact with and read environmental print in context.

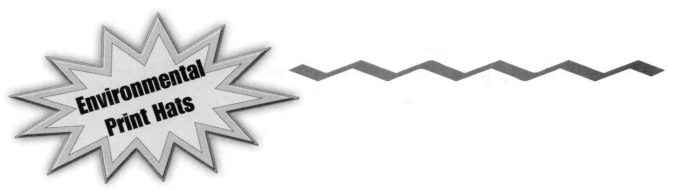

Objective:

Children will be able to read the environmental print on hats.

Materials and Construction:

- 12" x 20" (30.5 cm x 51 cm) sheets of plain newsprint (one sheet for each child)
- Environmental print from products
- Glue sticks
- Scissors

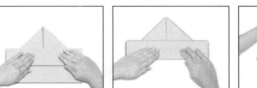

Fold the newsprint in half, making a "hamburger fold" with the opening at the bottom. Fold the top right corner to the middle. Fold the top left corner to the middle. Then, fold the bottom strips up on each side so that the opening is at the bottom. Have the children cut out environmental print that they can read and glue it onto the hat.

Procedures:

Plan an "Environmental Print Hat Day." Have children wear their hats during the day and read the print on their hats to each other. Ask children to find examples of environmental print they can read on other children's hats.

Adaptations:

- Make smaller environmental print hats for puppets or dolls in the classroom. Children can dress the puppets and dolls in the hats and read the print.
- Use a mitten pattern and cut out paper mittens. Glue environmental print on the mittens and use them as a bulletin board or clip the paper mittens on a clothesline hung in the classroom. Have children practice reading the print on the mittens.

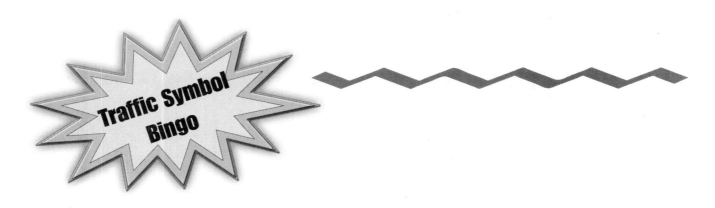

Objective:

Children will be able to identify the meanings of traffic symbols.

Materials and Construction:

- Computer
- Printer
- 8.5" x 11" (21.6 cm x 28 cm) printer paper
- Traffic signs with symbols
- 8.5" x 11" (21.6 cm x 28 cm) card stock
- Glue stick
- Marker
- Scissors
- Bingo chips
- Clear contact paper or laminating film
- One 2-quart (1.89 L) resealable, plastic bag for bingo cards
- One sandwich-size resealable, plastic bag for individual cards
- One sandwich-size resealable, plastic bag for bingo chips

To obtain traffic signs, go to a search engine such as Google®, AltaVista™, etc. Click on Images, type "traffic signs" in the search window, and then click Search. Select 15 traffic signs that have symbols to use on the bingo cards. Resize the images into 1.7" x 1.8" (4.3 cm x 4.6 cm) rectangles and print the images. Divide the 8.5" x 11" card stock into a 5 x 6 grid. In the first row of boxes, write B-I-N-G-O, with one letter in each box. Glue a traffic sign (symbol only) in each remaining box on the grid. Vary the placement of the signs to create different bingo cards. Make enough bingo cards for the children in your class or for the number of children you want to play the game (four to eight children, for example). Cut one bingo card apart to have individual traffic sign cards. Cover the bingo cards and individual traffic sign cards with clear contact paper or laminating film for durability. (See illustration on page 25.)

Procedures:

Give each child a bingo card and bingo chips. Select an individual traffic sign card and show it to the children. Have children cover the correct traffic sign. Any child with five chips in a row across, down, or diagonally should call out "Bingo!" The child must read the symbols to win.

Adaptations:

- Replace the word BINGO on the cards with the word LOTTO. Make individual cards to place over the symbols on the lotto card. Play as a lotto game. (For LOTTO directions, see Traffic Print Lotto, page 19.)
- Make two sets of individual symbol cards. Let children play concentration.

Objective:

Children will be able to identify the environmental print in a pocket chart.

Materials and Construction:

- Environmental print from products
- 5" x 8" (12.7 cm x 20.3 cm) unlined index cards
- Glue stick
- Scissors
- Clear contact paper or laminating film
- Pocket chart

Create environmental print cards by cutting labels off of various products and gluing them on the 5" x 8" (12.7 cm x 20.3 cm) unlined index cards. Cover the cards with clear contact paper or laminate for durability.

Procedures:

Hang the pocket chart where children can see and reach it. Place the environmental print cards in the chart, blank side out. Ask a child to go to the chart to select a card. Have the child read the environmental print on the selected card.

Adaptations:

- Ask one child to select the card from the pocket. Then, ask other children to volunteer to read the print.
- Use a carpenter's apron and put the environmental print in the pockets. Have one child wear the apron while other children select cards and read the print.

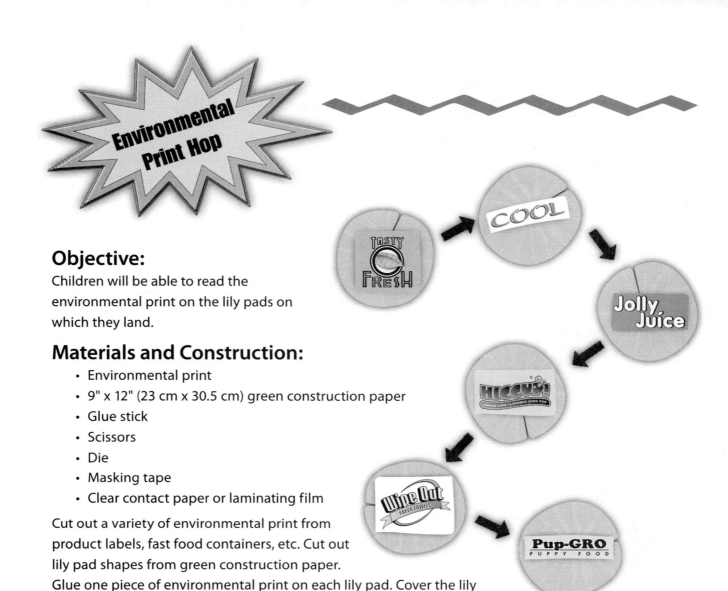

Objective:

Children will be able to read the environmental print on the lily pads on which they land.

Materials and Construction:

- Environmental print
- 9" x 12" (23 cm x 30.5 cm) green construction paper
- Glue stick
- Scissors
- Die
- Masking tape
- Clear contact paper or laminating film

Cut out a variety of environmental print from product labels, fast food containers, etc. Cut out lily pad shapes from green construction paper. Glue one piece of environmental print on each lily pad. Cover the lily pads with clear contact paper or laminating film for durability.

Procedures:

Put a rolled piece of masking tape on the back of each lily pad and secure it to the floor. Select four children to play the game. Have each child roll the die. The child with the highest number goes first. The first child rolls the die and counts the number of dots. The child must start at the first lily pad and hop the correct number of spaces. The child must read the print on the lily pad on which she lands. If the child cannot read the print, she must go back to the lily pad she was on before her roll. The next child takes a turn. The winner is the first child to reach the last lily pad.

Adaptations:

- Make individual cards that match the environmental print on the lily pads. Instead of rolling the die, have each child select a card and hop to the lily pad with the matching environmental print.
- Instead of taping the lily pads to the floor, glue the lily pads on a clear shower curtain. Cover the lily pads with clear contact paper. Play the game by rolling the die and hopping, or draw individual cards and play like Twister®.

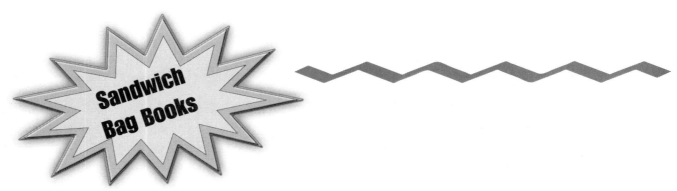

Objective:

Children will be able to read the environmental print in the Sandwich Bag Books.

Materials and Construction:

- Environmental print
- Card stock cut to fit inside sandwich-size resealable, plastic bags
- Glue stick
- Scissors
- Marker
- Yarn
- Large craft needle
- Sandwich-size resealable, plastic bags

Decide on the title of the book (for example, *Fruits We Love*). Cut out environmental print that fits the theme for the book. Glue the environmental print on card stock cut to fit inside the sandwich-size resealable, plastic bags. Then, place each environmental print card inside a bag to make the pages for the book. Create and place a title page in the first bag. Sew the bags together on the resealable (zipper) side.

Procedures:

Read the Sandwich Bag Books with children. Place the books in the reading area for children to read on their own.

Adaptations:

- Sew the resealable, plastic bags on the seam side. Change the environmental print in the Sandwich Bag Books as desired.
- Have children make a Sandwich Bag Book with the title *I Can Read*. Create books for each child using environmental print the child can read. Let children take the books home to read to their family members.

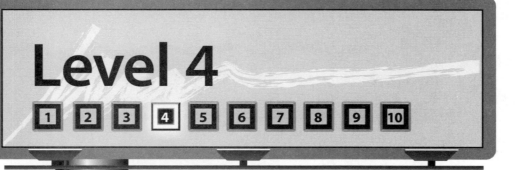

Level 4

Name Individual Letters

Main Objective:

Children will be able to identify and name individual letters.

Rationale:

Research shows that being able to name individual letters is a precursor to success in learning to read. Children need varied experiences in interacting with letters and learning the names of these letters.

The activities in this section begin with children finding and identifying letters in their names because this can be quite meaningful for them. Additional activities provide children with different types of experiences in naming individual letters.

**J for JELL-O®
and Jack**

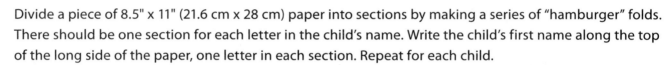

Objective:

Children will be able to identify letters in their names.

Materials and Construction:

- 8.5" x 11" (21.6 cm x 28 cm) paper
- Environmental print
- Glue sticks
- Marker
- Scissors

Divide a piece of 8.5" x 11" (21.6 cm x 28 cm) paper into sections by making a series of "hamburger" folds. There should be one section for each letter in the child's name. Write the child's first name along the top of the long side of the paper, one letter in each section. Repeat for each child.

Procedures:

Give children environmental print and ask them to find the individual letters in their names. Then, have them cut out the individual letters in their names. Children will glue these letters from the environmental print under the correct letters of their names on the folded paper.

Adaptations:

- Have children predict which letters they will find most or least often in the environmental print. Compare their answers to the results at the end of the activity.
- Once children have succeeded in finding letters for their first names, complete the same activity with letters for their last names.

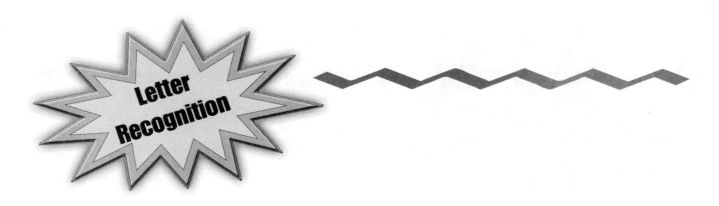

Objective:
Children will be able to identify letters in environmental print.

Materials and Construction:
- Environmental print
- Chart paper
- Glue stick
- Markers
- Scissors

Cut out environmental print from sources such as products, fast-food restaurant containers, and the Internet. Glue 8–10 pieces of environmental print on a piece of chart paper.

Procedures:
Gather children in a group on the floor in front of the chart. Ask children individually or as a group to read the names of the products. Then, ask individual children to come to the chart to find specific letters. Children may point to the letters or circle the letters with markers.

Adaptations:
- Use letter cards and have children find the matching letters on the chart.
- Have children find letters on the products that are in their names.

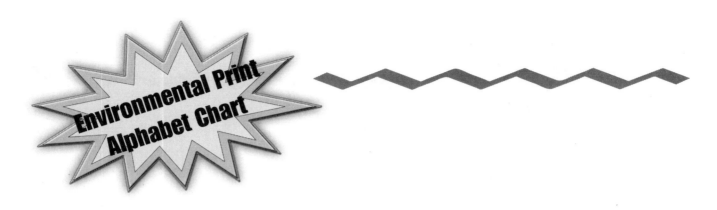

Objective:

Children will be able to identify and match the letters on the alphabet chart.

Materials and Construction:

- One 22" x 28" (56 cm x 71 cm) piece of poster board
- Environmental print
- Marker
- Ruler
- Glue sticks
- Scissors

Across the top of the poster board, write the title, "Environmental Print Alphabet Chart." Divide the poster board into 26 rectangles using a marker. Make the rectangles as large as possible. Write one letter of the alphabet in each rectangle.

Procedures:

Give children environmental print and ask them to cut out the individual letters. As they find individual letters, have them glue their letters onto the chart in the correct rectangles.

Adaptations:

- If children are not able to cut out the individual letters, let them pull precut environmental print letters from a bag and glue those to the chart.
- Give each child a specific letter to find for the chart. Then, supply children with environmental print samples to search for their assigned letters.

Objective:

Children will be able to place the environmental print "french fries" into the correct "french fry containers" using the first letter of the environmental print.

Materials and Construction:

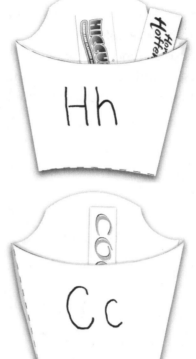

- 8.5" x 11" (21.6 cm x 28 cm) card stock
- Variety of environmental print
- Marker
- Glue stick
- Tape (optional)
- Scissors
- French fry container pattern (page 34)
- Clear contact paper or laminating film

Make four to six french fry containers (depending on the ability levels of your students) using the pattern (page 34). Trace the pattern onto card stock, then cut out. Glue or tape the pattern together along the sides to make french fry containers. Write a letter on each container. Find environmental print that begins with the letters written on the french fry containers and cut the print into strips to resemble french fries. These environmental print french fries can be glued onto card stock to make them more sturdy. Cover the environmental print french fries with clear contact paper or laminate for durability.

Procedures:

Place the french fry containers and environmental print french fries in the manipulatives center. Have children place the french fries into the correct containers according to the first letter of the environmental print.

Adaptations:

- Have children select the french fry containers that spell their names and find correct environmental print french fries for each container. Be sure to have enough containers for repeated letters (Tommy, Jennifer, etc.).
- Use real french fry containers from a favorite fast-food restaurant. Write the letters on pieces of paper and tape or glue them to the fronts of the containers. Cut french fry shapes from craft foam sheets (2 mm thick). Use a hot glue gun to glue environmental print onto the foam french fries.

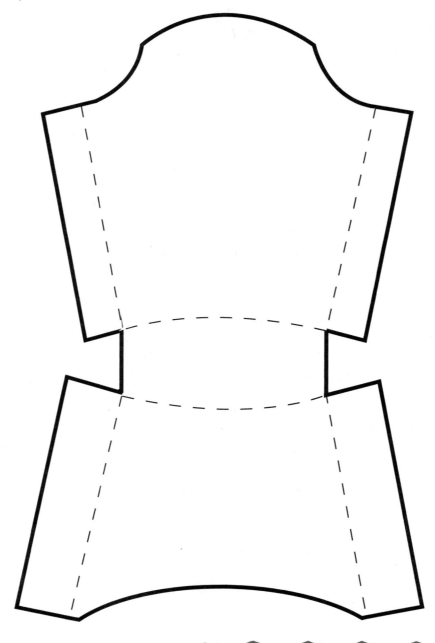

Objective:

Children will be able to name the letter the button lands on in the egg carton.

Materials and Construction:

- Egg carton
- Button or wooden bead
- Individual letters cut from environmental print
- Hot glue gun
- Scissors

Cut out individual letters from a variety of environmental print. Use a hot glue gun to glue each environmental print letter into the bottom of an egg carton cup.

Procedures:

Place a button or wooden bead into the egg carton and close the carton. Have children take turns shaking the carton and opening it to discover and name the letter in the cup in which the button or bead has landed.

Adaptations:

- Use letters that correspond with the first letters of children's names. This time when each child shakes the egg carton, he should try to get the button or bead to land in the cup that has his first initial in it. Use multiple egg cartons, if necessary.
- Cut out environmental print and glue onto 4" x 6" (10 cm x 15.24 cm) unlined index cards. Have children shake the egg carton with the button or bead in it. When each child opens the egg carton, she must identify the letter and find the card with environmental print that starts with the same letter.

Level 5

1 2 3 4 **5** 6 7 8 9 10

Level 5
Copy Print

Main Objective:
Children will be able to copy environmental print.

Rationale:
Because reading and writing develop simultaneously, children should have many opportunities to practice writing letters. These experiences should be meaningful for children.

The activities suggested for copying print offer children opportunities to copy print that is meaningful to them. They will have opportunities to use a variety of different writing materials, including a kinesthetic experience using Jell-O® Gelatin or other gelatin powder.

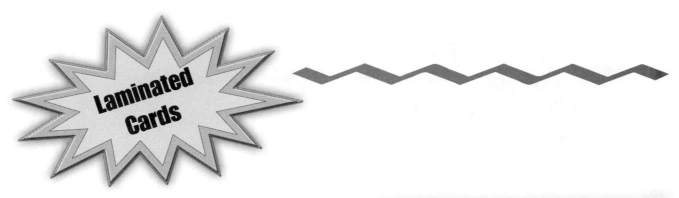

Objective:

Children will be able to trace over the environmental print on the laminated cards using a dry-erase marker.

Materials and Construction:

- Samples of environmental print with print large enough for children to trace
- 8.5" x 11" (21.6 cm x 28 cm) card stock
- Glue stick
- Scissors
- Clear contact paper or laminating film
- Dry-erase markers
- Paper towels

Cut the 8.5" x 11" card stock in half (8.5" x 5.5" or 21.6 cm x 14 cm). Glue environmental print to the card stock halves. Use clear contact paper or laminate environmental print cards for durability.

Procedures:

Allow children to trace letters using dry-erase markers. These are easily wiped off with wet or dry paper towels and ready to be reused. Use a variety of environmental print including both uppercase and lowercase letters when making the cards.

Adaptations:

- Use a dry-erase marker to trace over the print on juice pouches like Capri Sun® and Kool-Aid®. The marker will wipe right off of the surface of the pouches.
- Place the environmental print cards under the clear sheet on a Magic Slate® or other self-erasing slate. Trace over the environmental print using the stylus that comes with the slate. Be sure to press hard. Remove the card to see the print on the slate.

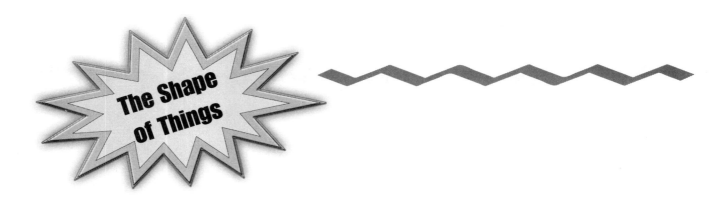

Objective:

Children will be able to trace over the environmental print found on traffic and street signs.

Materials and Construction:

- 8.5" x 11" (21.6 cm x 28 cm) card stock
- Printouts of traffic and street signs from the Internet
- Dry-erase or water-soluble markers
- Clear contact paper or laminating film
- Paper towels

To obtain traffic signs, go to an online search engine such as Google®, AltaVista™, etc. Click on Images, type "traffic signs" in the search window, and then click Search. Select and print the traffic and street signs desired on the card stock. Cut out the signs and cover with clear contact paper or laminate for durability.

Procedures:

Place the traffic and street signs in the Writing Center. Give children dry-erase markers to trace over the letters. Place paper towels in the Writing Center. Have children use dry paper towels to wipe off dry-erase markers and damp paper towels to wipe off the water-soluble markers.

Adaptations:

- Create street signs to trace with the names of streets the children live on.
- Cartoon titles are often written with a defined shape around them. Cut these out, glue on card stock, cover with clear contact paper or laminate, and let the children trace over the letters.

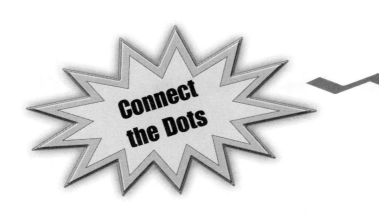

Objective:

Children will be able to trace over the dots to copy the environmental print.

Materials and Construction:

- 8.5" x 11" (21.6 cm x 28 cm) card stock
- Environmental print
- Computer
- Printer
- Markers
- Glue stick
- Clear contact paper or laminating film
- Dry-erase markers
- Paper towels

Make "I Can Read and Write" cards using environmental print for words that children can read and write. Print the words "I can read and write." in a large font on several pieces of 8.5" x 11" (21.6 cm x 28 cm) card stock. Glue a copy of the environmental print below the words "I can read and write." Draw a dotted outline of each word for children to trace over. Cover with clear contact paper or laminate.

Procedures:

Work with three or four children at one time. Have the small group sit at a table with you. Ask children to read the cards. After they read the cards, let children trace over the environmental print. Tracing lines can be wiped off with paper towels. After all children have had an opportunity to work with you, place the "I Can Read and Write" cards in the Writing Center.

Adaptations:

- Print "I Can Read and Write" cards on regular printer paper. Add environmental print by importing images from the Internet or gluing the environmental print below the typed phrase. Add the dotted outline. Children can trace these and take them home to share with their families.
- Space the dots further apart as children's skills improve until no dots are necessary.

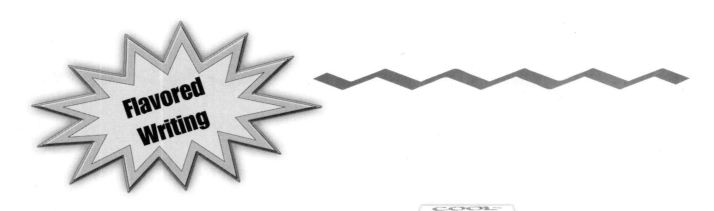

Objective:

Children will be able to write the flavor of the gelatin in the gelatin powder.

Materials and Construction:

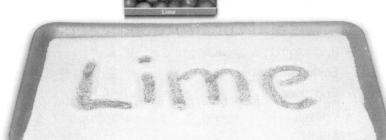

- Jell-O® Gelatin powder or other gelatin powder
- Trays or plastic containers with sides

Pour the gelatin powder on the tray or plastic container. Place the empty gelatin box next to the tray.

Procedures:

Work with small groups of children to introduce this activity. Show children the empty gelatin box. Point out the flavor name and have children name the letters. Then, have children copy the flavor name in the gelatin powder. Remind children not to eat the powder. This activity can be used later as a free choice selection.

Adaptations:

- Use dry pudding mix, salt, flour, or other dry ingredients in which the children can write environmental print.
- Give children finger paints: red for cherry-flavored gelatin, green for lime-flavored gelatin, etc. Let them use their fingers, cotton swabs, or paint brushes to copy the flavor names onto paper.

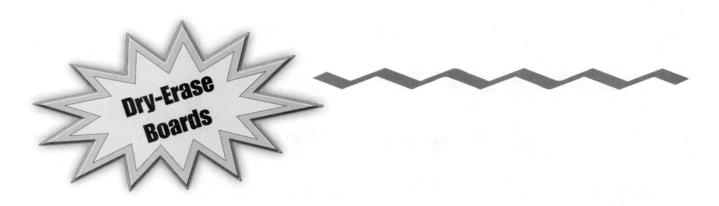

Dry-Erase Boards

Objective:

Children will be able to copy the environmental print onto dry-erase boards.

Materials and Construction:

- Individual dry-erase boards
- Dry-erase markers
- Dry-erase board erasers
- Variety of environmental print
- 5" x 8" (12.7 cm x 20.3 cm) unlined index cards
- Glue stick
- Scissors
- Clear contact paper or laminating film
- Baskets or plastic containers for storage

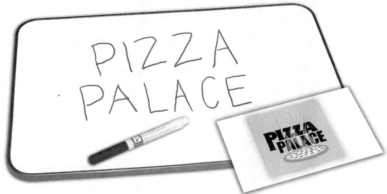

Collect samples of environmental print. Glue the print onto 5" x 8" (12.7 cm x 20.3 cm) unlined index cards. Cover the cards with clear contact paper or laminate for durability.

Procedures:

Supply children with dry-erase boards, a selection of markers, and a variety of environmental print that they can copy onto the dry-erase boards. The environmental print can be stored in baskets or plastic containers from which children are free to choose the print they would like to copy. Include a variety of environmental print such as cereal boxes, labels from snack foods, and characters and titles from familiar cartoons. Be sure to include uppercase and lowercase letters to copy.

Adaptations:

- Chalk is also a medium children can use. Supply a small chalkboard and colorful chalk for environmental print writing.
- Provide a magnetic drawing board on which the children can write environmental print with the magnetic pen.

Level 6
Match Decontextualized Words

Main Objective:

Children will be able to recognize decontextualized environmental print and match it to environmental print in context.

Rationale:

Initially, children read environmental print by associating it with the colors, shape, and pictures. It is more difficult to read the print when it is removed from this context. Children need to have experiences reading environmental print in decontextualized settings.

The activities in this section provide a variety of appropriate experiences to introduce children to reading decontextualized environmental print.

Objective:

Children will be able to place pillows with decontextualized words onto the correct environmental print quilt squares.

Materials and Construction:

- 6" x 6" (15.24 cm x 15.24 cm) squares of card stock
- Scissors
- Ruler
- Glue stick
- Tape
- Variety of environmental print
- Marker

Cut out 6" x 6" (15.24 cm x 15.24 cm) squares of card stock. Glue environmental print to each square. Tape the squares together to make a "quilt." Cut out 6" x 6" (15.24 cm x 15.24 cm) squares of paper to make "pillows" for each square in the quilt. Write the environmental print from the quilt on the pillows (one pillow for each square on the quilt). Each pillow will have decontextualized environmental print written on it.

Procedures:

Have children sit in a circle on the floor. Place the environmental print quilt in the center of the circle. Place the decontextualized environmental print pillows around the outside of the quilt. Ask children to select decontextualized environmental print pillows and find the correct environmental print quilt squares on which to place them.

Adaptations:

- Secure the quilt to a wall and attach the pillows to the correct quilt squares with adhesive magnet strips or hook-and-loop tape.
- One adaptation that is time consuming (but worth the effort) is to make an environmental print fabric quilt. First, find environmental print on the Internet and use an iron-on transfer computer package to create iron-on squares of the print. Iron the various pieces of environmental print onto pieces of fabric. Sew the fabric pieces together to make a quilt. The pillows can be made by using a word-processing program and printing the decontextualized environmental print on iron-on transfer paper. Iron each piece of decontextualized environmental print onto a piece of fabric. Cut a second piece of the same fabric for the backing. Sew the two pieces together and stuff with polyester fiberfill to make a pillow. Continue until you have pillows to cover all of the environmental print on the quilt.

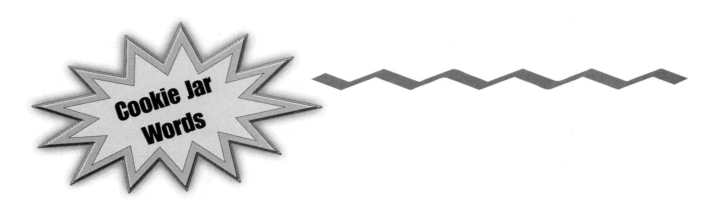

Cookie Jar Words

Objective:

Children will be able to place decontextualized "cookies" into the correct environmental print cookie jars.

Materials and Construction:

- Plastic milk or juice jugs
- Variety of cereal boxes
- Scissors
- Marker
- Glue or tape
- Card stock
- Clear contact paper or laminating film

Cut the tops off of plastic milk or juice jugs to create cookie jars.

Cut the cereal logos/names from various cereal boxes. Glue or tape a logo/name to the front of each milk or juice jug.

Cut card stock circles (cookies) that will fit inside the "cookie jars." Using a marker, write the names of the cereals from the cookie jars on the card stock "cookies." Make four or five cookies for each jar. To make the cookies more durable, cover with clear contact paper or laminate.

Procedures:

Work with a small group of children. Have the group sit at a table. Place the cookie jars on the table with the cereal logo/name facing the children. Shuffle the cookies, then lay them on the table with the cereal names facing up. Ask children to select cookies that they can read and place them in the correct cookie jars. As children become more familiar with matching the decontextualized words to the environmental print, you can place the cookies on the table with the cereal names facedown. Have children select cookies, turn them over, read the names, and place them in the correct cookie jars.

Adaptations:

- Use environmental print cookie jars and decontextualized cookies to play a group game. Have children sit in a circle with the cookie jars in the middle of the circle. Let players pass one cookie around the circle while singing the line "Who stole the cookie from the cookie jar?" The child with the cookie when the word "jar" is sung must put the "stolen" cookie back into the correct cookie jar. That player then chooses a new cookie to pass around the circle.
- For another small group game, give each child an environmental print cookie jar. Spread the decontextualized cookies out facedown on the playing surface. Have players take turns trying to find cookies for their cookie jars.

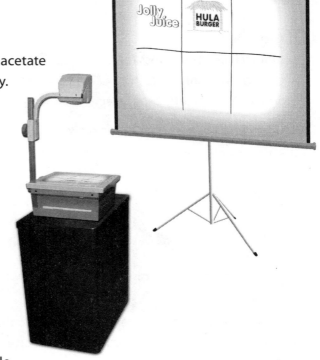

Objective:

Children will be able to match the decontextualized acetate cards to the environmental print on the transparency.

Materials and Construction:

- Transparency film
- 8.5" x 11" (21.6 cm x 28 cm) paper
- Variety of environmental print
- Scissors
- Glue stick
- Marker
- Ruler
- Copier or computer and printer
- Overhead projector

Divide an 8.5" x 11" (21.6 cm x 28 cm) piece of paper into six to nine rectangles. Cut out environmental print and glue one piece of print into each rectangle. Copy the page onto transparency film.

To create a transparency on a computer, use a word-processing program. Divide an 8.5" x 11" (21.6 cm x 28 cm) page into six to nine squares. Import one piece of environmental print in each square. Print the environmental print on transparency film.

Cut a sheet of transparency film into rectangles the same size as those on the environmental print transparency. Write the decontextualized words on the individual transparency rectangles to match the environmental print on the transparency.

Procedures:

Place the transparency on the overhead projector and have children read the environmental print. Then, have a child select a transparency rectangle with decontextualized print and place it on the correct environmental print on the transparency.

Adaptation:

- Make individual letters on 2" x 2" (5 cm x 5 cm) acetate cards. Children must find the individual letters to spell out the words on environmental print.

Objective:

Children will be able to toss (or drop) beanbags onto the correct environmental print cards based on the decontextualized cards they select.

Materials and Construction:

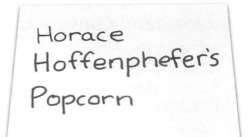

- Variety of environmental print
- 8.5" x 11" (21.6 cm x 28 cm) card stock
- Ruler
- Glue stick
- Scissors
- Marker
- Clear contact paper or laminating film
- Beanbags

Cut out a variety of environmental print. Cut an 8.5" x 11" (21.6 cm x 28 cm) piece of card stock into 4.25" x 5.5" (10.75 cm x 14 cm) rectangles and glue one sample of environmental print on each card. Write the decontextualized print on separate pieces of card stock (4.25" x 5.5"/10.75 cm x 14 cm). Cover all of the cards with clear contact paper or laminate for durability.

Procedures:

Spread the rectangles with the environmental print out on the floor. Have children pick decontextualized print cards from a pile. Children must read the decontextualized print and attempt to toss (or drop) beanbags onto the matching environmental print rectangles.

Adaptations:

- Tape environmental print onto the bottoms of plastic bins. Let children attempt to toss the beanbags into the baskets that match the decontextualized print cards instead of aiming for rectangles.
- Glue environmental print onto the inside bottoms of empty shoe boxes. Children can roll tennis balls into shoe boxes containing the environmental print that matches their decontextualized cards.

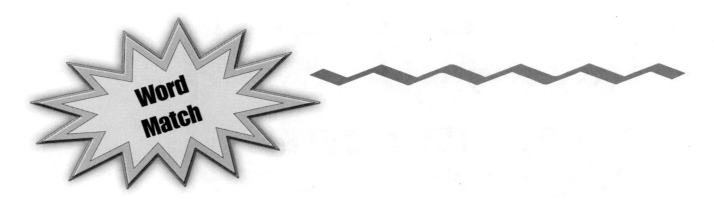

Objective:
Children will be able to match decontextualized print with words in context.

Materials and Construction:
- Variety of environmental print
- 5" x 8" (12.7 cm x 20.3 cm) unlined index cards
- Markers
- Scissors
- Glue stick
- Clear contact paper or laminating film

Cut out environmental print and glue it onto 5" x 8" (12.7 cm x 20.3 cm) unlined index cards. Write the decontextualized print on separate 5" x 8" (12.7 cm x 20.3 cm) unlined index cards using a marker. Cover the cards with clear contact paper or laminate for durability.

Procedures:
Place the environmental print cards on a table. Next to these cards, place the decontextualized print cards. Have a child select a card with the decontextualized environmental print. The child must match the decontextualized word to the environmental print card and read the word.

Adaptations:
- Use the Word Match cards to play concentration.
- Have children match beginning letters instead of complete words.

Level 7

1 **2** **3** **4** **5** **6** **7** **8** **9** **10**

Level 7
Classify by Category

Main Objective:
Children will be able to classify environmental print using various criteria.

Rationale:
Since classification skills are important to literacy and mathematics, children should have numerous opportunities to sort objects. Environmental print can be used to provide children with experiences in classification.

The activities in this section begin with broad classification experiences and move to more refined classifications. These experiences provide children with opportunities to interact with environmental print in problem-solving situations. Classification activities require children to determine the common attributes among given items.

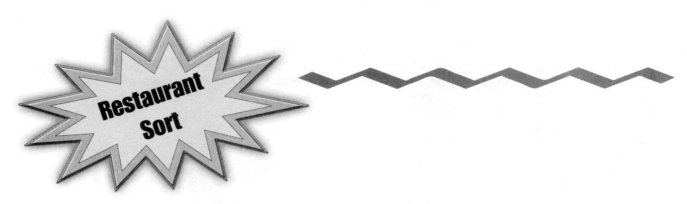

Objective:

Children will be able to sort restaurant cards into the correct boxes.

Materials and Construction:

- Logos of restaurants from paper bags
- Card stock
- Scissors
- Glue stick
- Five empty shoe boxes
- Clear contact paper or laminating film
- Decorative contact paper

Select five different restaurants and obtain paper bags with the restaurants' logos. Cut the restaurants' logos from the paper bags. Glue the logos on 8.5" x 5.5" (21.6 cm x 14 cm) pieces of card stock. Make six cards for each restaurant for a total of 30 cards. Cover the restaurant cards with clear contact paper or laminate for durability.

Cover five empty shoe boxes with decorative contact paper. Use a glue stick to attach one copy of each restaurant card to the front of each shoe box.

Procedures:

Introduce the sorting activity to small groups of children. Ask children to name the restaurant on each shoe box. Then, show them the individual restaurant cards. Explain that the object is to place the cards in the correct shoe boxes. Shuffle the cards and place them facedown on a table. Have one child pick up the top card, identify the restaurant, and place the card in the correct box. Let each child take a turn.

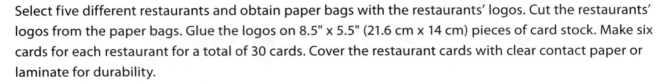

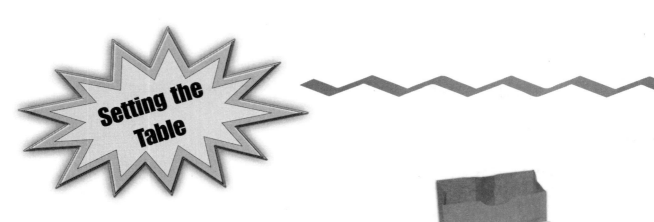

Setting the Table

Objective:

Children will be able to classify environmental print according to three food/drink categories: served on a plate, served in a bowl, and served in a cup.

Materials and Construction:

- One paper grocery bag
- One paper plate, one paper bowl, and one paper cup
- Variety of environmental print from foods served on plates (pizza, lunch meat, hot dogs, cheese, cookies, etc.), foods that are served in bowls (cereal, Jell-O® Gelatin, soup, etc.), food served in cups (Kool-Aid®, lemonade, juice, etc.)
- 3" x 5" (7.6 cm x 12.7 cm) and/or 4" x 6" (10 cm x 15.24 cm) unlined index cards
- Scissors
- Glue stick
- Clear contact paper or laminating film

Cut out a variety of environmental print from various food products. Be sure to include food served on plates, food served in bowls, and food served in cups. Glue the environmental print onto index cards. Cover cards with clear contact paper or laminate.

Procedures:

Gather a small group of children together at a table. Ask them to identify the various product labels/logos. Place the environmental print into a grocery bag. Direct children to set the table by selecting environmental print from the grocery bag and placing each piece in the container from which it would be served: plate, bowl, or cup. Children should continue the process until all of the food products are sorted.

Adaptations:

- Have children select one product label from each container to display their favorite lunch or dinner.
- Have children name all of the food products featured that they have eaten.

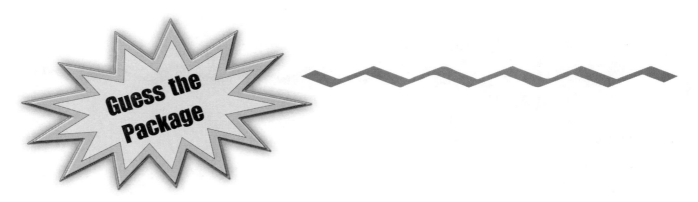

Objective:

Children will be able to sort food labels/logos by the way they are packaged.

Materials and Construction:

- One large, empty can with label (for example, a commercial-size can of peaches)
- One empty cereal box
- Variety of environmental print from canned goods and boxed products
- 4" x 6" (10 cm x 15.24 cm) unlined index cards
- Scissors
- Glue stick
- Masking tape (optional)
- Clear contact paper or laminating film

Cut the environmental print from canned goods and products packaged in boxes. Glue the logos/labels on index cards. Cover with clear contact paper or laminate for durability. Thoroughly wash and dry a large, empty can. If necessary, use masking tape to cover any sharp edges at the top of the can to prevent children from cutting themselves. Cut the top off of the empty cereal box.

Procedures:

This activity can be completed with a small or large group of children. Gather children together. Have children identify the products on the environmental print cards. Shuffle the cards and lay them facedown. Place the empty can and box in front of the children. Have one child pick up the top environmental print card, identify the product, and place the card in the can or box, depending upon how the product is usually packaged. Let children continue to read the environmental print cards and place them in the can or in the box according to how they are packaged at the store until all cards have been sorted.

Adaptations:

- Use paper grocery bags instead of the can and cereal box. Label one bag "Cans" and the other "Boxes." Have children sort the environmental print cards into the grocery bags based on how the products are packaged.
- Using a variety of environmental print cards, children can sort products by whether they are refrigerated, frozen, or stored on shelves.

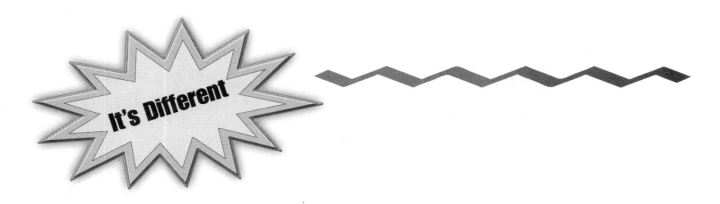

Objective:

Children will be able to select the piece of environmental print that does not belong in the same category with three other products.

Materials and Construction:

- Variety of environmental print
- 5" x 8" (12.7 cm x 20.3 cm) unlined index cards
- Scissors
- Glue stick
- Clear contact paper or laminating film
- Lunch bags (paper or reusable)

Collect various pieces of environmental print. Include store and restaurant logos, traffic signs, and product labels. Cut out the environmental print and glue on 5" x 8" (12.7 cm x 20.3 cm) unlined index cards. Cover with clear contact paper or laminate for durability.

Procedures:

Introduce this activity to small groups of children. Place four cards in various lunch bags. Three of the cards should have something in common; one card will not belong ("it's different"). For example, place three cereal box fronts and one soup label in a bag, three restaurant logos and one traffic sign in another bag, etc. Have a child select a bag with the product cards. Ask the child to pull out the cards (one at a time), name the products, and place the cards face up on the table or floor. Ask the child to find the one product that does not belong with the others. Have the child explain why that product is different and does not belong.

Adaptations:

- As children become more familiar with this game, encourage them to play with partners.
- Make the game more challenging by creating more refined discriminations. For example, include three cold cereal box fronts and one hot cereal box front. Children should choose the hot cereal because "it's different."

Objective:

Children will be able to select only the breakfast food environmental print from a collection of food labels/logos and glue them onto a cardboard-box car.

Materials and Construction:

- Variety of environmental print from breakfast, lunch, and dinner foods
- Three cardboard boxes of different sizes
- Brass fasteners
- Scissors
- Glue sticks
- Black tempera paint
- Paint brush

To construct a car from the cardboard boxes, glue a smaller box to the top of a larger box to form the outline of a car. Cut four cardboard circles (wheels) from the remaining box. The size of the wheels will depend on the sizes of the boxes used to make the car. Paint the wheels black and attach them to the car using brass fasteners.

Procedures:

Have children sort through a variety of food-related environmental print and select those labels and logos for breakfast foods. Have children glue the breakfast food environmental print onto the car to create a Breakfastmobile. After the Breakfastmobile is completed, have children name the various products.

Adaptations:

- Have children make a Lunchmobile or Dinnermobile.
- Use poster board or paper to make a two-dimensional Breakfastmobile. Draw the outline of a car and have children glue breakfast food environmental print inside the outline.

Level 8

1 2 3 4 5 6 7 8 9 10

Level 8
Dictate Stories

Main Objective:
Children will be able to use environmental print in stories they dictate or sentences they complete.

Rationale:
Transcribing children's oral language into print is a powerful way to encourage them to read. Children are excited about seeing their words in print. This text is meaningful to children. Sentences and stories that contain environmental print encourage literacy in young children.

The activities in this section provide opportunities for children to dictate sentences and stories throughout the day. The complexity of the activities varies and supports children's abilities to use environmental print in dictation.

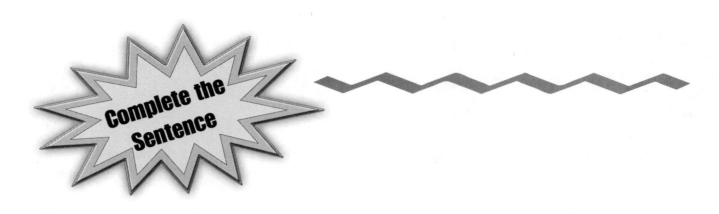

Objective:

Children will be able to select the appropriate environmental print to complete sentences.

Materials and Construction:

- Sentence strips
- Marker
- Variety of environmental print
- 4" x 6" (10 cm x 15.24 cm) unlined index cards
- Glue stick
- Scissors
- Strip magnets or hook-and-loop tape

Cut out examples of environmental print that children can read. Glue the environmental print onto 4" x 6" (10 cm x 15.24 cm) unlined index cards. Place a piece of strip magnet or hook-and-loop tape on the back of each index card. Write three to four sentences on sentence strips (depending on the ability of children), leaving a blank space for the children to fill in with an environmental print word. Place a piece of the strip magnet or hook-and-loop tape on the blank space to attach the environmental print word card.

Procedures:

Read the sentences, one at a time, to children. Choose one child to select an environmental print word card to attach to the blank space. Have a variety of environmental print words from which children can choose. Together with children, reread the sentence with the environmental print word included.

Adaptations:

- Write the sentences on chart paper.
- Have a small group play a matching sentences game. Give each child copies of the environmental print cards that can be used to fill in the blanks in sentences. All of the children will have the same environmental print. Write a sentence on chart paper such as, "Dylan is so silly, he ate _____ for dinner." Turn the chart paper away from children so that they cannot see what environmental print word will be used to fill in the blank. Have one child fill in the blank while the others guess which environmental print word will be chosen. Have children place all of their environmental print cards facedown except for the card they think has been used to fill in the blank. Turn the chart paper around to see how many matches there are.

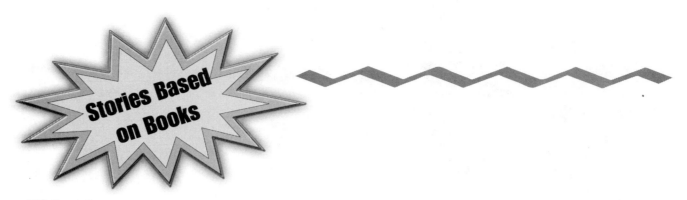

Stories Based on Books

Objective:

Children will be able to select environmental print to "rewrite" a familiar story.

Materials and Construction:

- Book to adapt
- Variety of environmental print
- Chart paper
- Markers
- Glue stick
- Scissors

Select a book that lends itself to adaptation, such as *Brown Bear, Brown Bear, What Do You See?* (Bill Martin Jr., Henry Holt and Co., 1992). Write the story on chart paper using a marker. Keep the main idea of the story while leaving blank spaces where environmental print can be substituted.

Procedures:

Gather children together in front of the chart paper. Read the original book. Then, explain to children that they will rewrite the story using environmental print to replace parts of the story. Show them the story rewritten on chart paper. Read the story and stop when you get to a blank space where environmental print can be substituted. Show children the samples of environmental print. Ask a child to select one of the environmental print words to place in the story. Glue the environmental print in place. Continue until the story is complete. A new version of *Brown Bear, Brown Bear, What Do You See?* for example, could include "I see Sam holding Kix® for me."

Adaptations:

- Give each child one of the environmental print words used in the chart paper story. Read the chart paper story aloud. If a child hears the environmental print word he has, he should hold it up for everyone to see.
- Make books from the new stories. Write or type the story text and glue the environmental print where it fits in the story. Have children illustrate the pages. Staple the pages together to make a book.

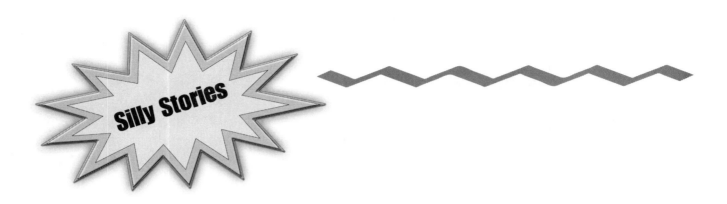

Silly Stories

Objective:

Children will be able to randomly select environmental print to create a story.

Materials and Construction:

- Book to adapt
- Chart paper
- Marker
- Variety of environmental print
- 4" x 6" (10 cm x 15.24 cm) unlined index cards
- Glue stick
- Scissors
- Tape
- Paper lunch bag

Cut out environmental print and glue onto the 4" x 6" (10 cm x 15.24 cm) unlined index cards. Place the cards in the paper lunch bag. Select a familiar book, such as *The Bag I'm Taking to Grandma's* (Shirley Neitzel, HarperTrophy, 1998). Rewrite the story on chart paper, drawing blank lines where nouns would be.

Procedures:

Gather children together and review the original story. Explain that they will help you to write a silly story. Show children the chart and read the story until you come to a blank line. Have one child come up, draw an environmental print card from the paper bag, and tape it on the first blank line in the story. Continue until all of the blank lines are full. Reread the new story and listen to the children's laughter as they hear their silly story.

Adaptations:

- Have children find environmental print that would make sense in the story.
- Use environmental print to rewrite a poem.

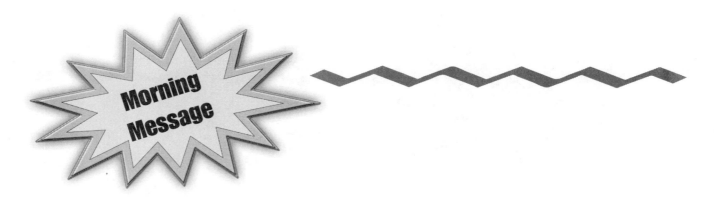

Objective:

Children will be able to select environmental print and use it in a meaningful context.

Materials and Construction:

- Variety of environmental print
- 4" x 6" (10 cm x 15.24 cm) unlined index cards
- Craft sticks
- Scissors
- Glue stick
- Tape

Cut out environmental print from various sources. Include store, restaurant, and cartoon character logos. Glue the environmental print onto 4" x 6" (10 cm x 15.24 cm) unlined index cards. Tape these cards to craft sticks.

Procedures:

As part of morning message time, choose children to come up and select environmental print craft sticks and then share stories about them. One child may tell you, "I'm going to McDonald's® after school, and I'm getting a chocolate milk shake." This allows children to share something about their lives outside of school (which they love to do) and put the environmental print into a meaningful context.

Adaptation:

- Create environmental print craft sticks with food items only. Write "I like to eat _____." as part of the morning message. Have children select the food items they like to eat and complete the sentence.
- Ask children to select a set number of environmental print craft sticks; start with two and increase the number. Have children dictate sentences that include the environmental print on the sticks. Write the sentences on the board or chart paper and read as part of the morning message.

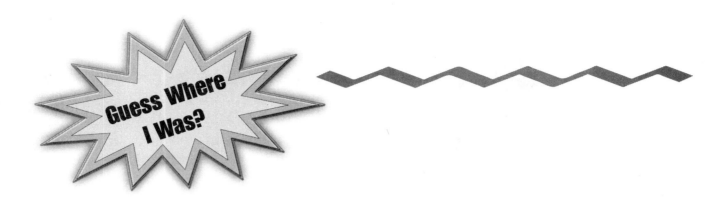

Objective:

Using environmental print and picture clues, children will be able to tell a story about a retail store and have listeners identify the store.

Materials and Construction:

- Paper lunch bags
- Environmental print featuring retail store names
- Pictures and environmental print featuring items that can be found in retail stores
- Tape

Cut out pictures and environmental print featuring items that can be found in retail stores. Place pictures and environmental print of items that can be found at the same retail store into a paper lunch bag. (Begin with three stores and increase the number as children's skill levels improve.) On the bottom of the bag, tape environmental print with the name of the store where these items can be found. Continue until you have filled and labeled all of the paper lunch bags.

Procedures:

Gather a small group of children. Introduce the activity by modeling. Begin to tell your story by saying, "I went to the store and bought _____," filling in the blank by pulling an item from the bag to tell what you bought. Continue until all of the items in the bag have been used. When the story is finished, ask the children to guess the name of the store. After modeling the activity, ask children, one at a time, to select a bag and tell stories to the other children.

Adaptation:

- Tape the pictures and environmental print of the store items to the outside of the bag. Place the environmental print logo of the store inside the bag. Children can look at the bags, guess the store's name, and check their answers.

Level 9

Classify by Initial Sounds

Main Objective:

Children will be able to classify environmental print by matching initial sounds.

Rationale:

Children need many experiences working with the individual sounds of spoken words. Phonemic awareness is critical to children learning to read. Once children have had experiences listening to and identifying the sounds of letters in spoken words, they can begin to associate the sounds with the written letters.

The experiences in this section provide children with opportunities to classify environmental print according to its initial sound and match that sound to the correct letter. These experiences will help children develop an understanding of the alphabetic principle—the systematic and predictable relationships between written letters and spoken sounds. Such an understanding has been shown to contribute to children's literacy development.

Objective:

Children will be able to classify coupons according to the beginning sound of the product name.

Materials and Construction:

- Assortment of store, newspaper, and product coupons
- 5–10 sheets of paper
- Paper lunch bag or manila envelope
- Marker
- Scissors
- Glue sticks
- Stapler

Create a 5–10 page Coupon Scrapbook by writing letter sounds with which students are familiar. Put one letter sound on each page, and write both an uppercase and lowercase letter at the top of each page. Staple the pages together. Collect an assortment of coupons with product names that begin with the same letter sounds as those in the booklet. Put the coupons in a paper lunch bag or manila envelope.

Procedures:

Review the letter sounds included in the booklet by having children name each one. Show them the assortment of coupons and model sounding out the beginning sounds. For example, using a Kix® coupon helps children identify the /k/ sound and place it on the Kk page. Instruct children to identify the sounds and glue all of the coupons on the correct pages.

Adaptations:

- Allow children to bring the Coupon Scrapbook home to read to their parents. Encourage them to find and add additional coupons at home.
- Glue coupons onto index cards or card stock cut to the appropriate size. Cover with clear contact paper or laminate, then add hook-and-loop tape to the back of the coupons. Make individual letter pages on poster board. Add hook-and-loop tape to attach the coupons.

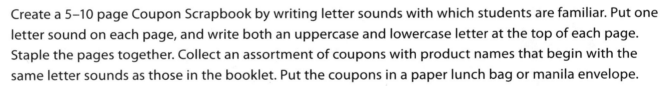

Clothesline

Objective:

Children will be able to classify product labels/logos by placing them on the clothesline with clothespins that have the matching beginning letter sounds.

Materials and Construction:

- Assortment of environmental print
- Clothespins
- Clothesline
- 5" x 8" (12.7 cm x 20.3 cm) unlined index cards
- Marker
- Scissors
- Glue stick
- Clear contact paper or laminating film

Cut out an assortment of environmental print (product labels, logos, signs, etc.). Glue each piece of environmental print onto a 5" x 8" (12.7 cm x 20.3 cm) unlined index card. Cover each card with clear contact paper or laminate for durability. Hang the clothesline so that children will be able to reach it. (Caution: Be sure to hang the clothesline in a place where children will not get hurt.) Write a letter on each clothespin with a marker. Prepare a clothespin for every letter, except X. Introduce the activity with four to five letters and increase that number as children's abilities increase.

Procedures:

Demonstrate how to classify the beginning letter sound of an environmental print word by sounding it out and then attaching it to the clothesline using the clothespin with the matching letter. Have children take turns sounding out the beginning letters of the environmental print cards and hanging them on the clothesline with the appropriate lettered clothespins.

Adaptations:

- Attach magnets to the backs of the clothespins. Have children clip all of the cards that begin with a specific letter to the clothespin with the corresponding letter and place it on a white board or other metal display surface.
- Encourage children to chant their matches to you (for example, a = applesauce, b = beans, etc.).

Objective:

Children will be able to classify a variety of environmental print by beginning letter sounds.

Materials and Construction:

- Variety of environmental print (product labels, logos, signs, etc.)
- 3" x 5" (7.6 cm x 12.7 cm) unlined index cards
- Manila folders
- Scissors
- Glue stick
- Marker

Open a manila folder. At the top left side of the folder, write a letter in uppercase and lowercase. On the top right side of the folder, write a different letter in uppercase and lowercase. Prepare folders for all of the initial letter sounds. Cut out a variety of environmental print (product labels, logos, signs, etc.) and glue onto 3" x 5" (7.6 cm x 12.7 cm) unlined index cards.

Procedures:

Begin with one folder (two letters) and only include environmental print that begins with those letters. Show children how each folder has been divided into two sections. Ask children to identify each letter. Select one environmental print card. Have children identify the environmental print label. Model how to classify the label by sounding out the beginning letter sound with the children and placing the label on the correct side of the folder. Ask children to select another card and identify the initial sound. Continue until all cards have been sorted. Once children are familiar with the activity, place the folder in a center to be used individually or in small groups. Increase the number of folders/letters as children's skills improve, but limit the activity to four to six letters.

Adaptations:

- Divide the folders into three or more sections depending on the abilities of your students.
- Instead of having children look at the environmental print cards, say the words aloud. Ask children with which of the two letters the environmental print begins. Then, show the card to the children.

Objective:

Children will be able to classify environmental print by beginning sounds.

Materials and Construction:

- Cookie sheet
- Magnetic letters
- Roll of magnetic tape
- Variety of environmental print (product labels, logos, signs, etc.)
- 3" x 5" (7.6 cm x 12.7 cm) unlined index cards
- Scissors
- Glue stick
- Clear contact paper or laminating film

Collect a variety of environmental print (product labels, logos, signs, etc.). Glue each piece of environmental print on a 3" x 5" (7.6 cm x 12.7 cm) index card and attach a strip of magnetic tape to the back. Cover the cards with clear contact paper or laminate for durability.

Procedures:

Work with a small group of children. Choose two magnetic letters and place them on the cookie sheet. Lay out the environmental print cards. Children will take turns selecting an environmental print card, identifying the product, and classifying it by placing the card on the cookie sheet next to the magnetic letter with the correct beginning sound.

Adaptations:

- Increase the number of letters to three or more, depending on the abilities of your children.
- Use a large six-cup muffin pan and have children work with partners to classify the environmental print. Use a hot glue gun to glue each environmental print letter into the bottom of a muffin cup. (Do not put the labels/logos on cards if using the muffin pan.)

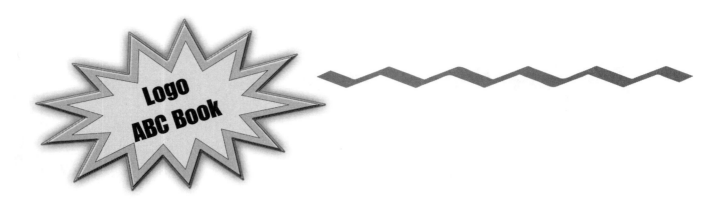

Logo ABC Book

Objective:

Children will be able to classify environmental print by beginning sounds.

Materials and Construction:

- Variety of environmental print (product labels, logos, signs, etc.)
- 11" x 17" (28 cm x 43 cm) paper
- Marker
- Scissors
- Glue sticks

Construct a blank ABC book by stapling 26 11" x 17" (28 cm x 43 cm) pages together. Print one letter in uppercase and one in lowercase on each page.

Procedure:

Invite children to create a large, classroom Logo ABC Book. Ask children to cut out individual pieces of environmental print. Have them glue each piece of environmental print onto the page in the book that has the same beginning letter. Place the book in the reading center or class library.

Adaptations:

- Make individual books for the children. Vary the number of pages by including only the letters with which each child is familiar.
- Make individual "Name Books" by writing one letter of a child's name at the top of each page. Instruct the child to paste environmental print that begins with the same letter as the letters in her name on each page of the book.

Level 10

Level 10
Classify by Syllables

Main Objective:
Children will be able to identify the number of syllables in words and classify environmental print by the number of syllables in the words.

Rationale:
Before children can identify syllables in words, they need to have many experiences playing with words. When they are ready to begin to identify syllables, children need opportunities to practice this skill in a variety of ways. Segmenting words into syllables is part of phonological awareness which helps children learn to read.

The activities in this section provide children with various ways to identify syllables in environmental print. Children are provided with kinesthetic experiences to help them recognize syllables.

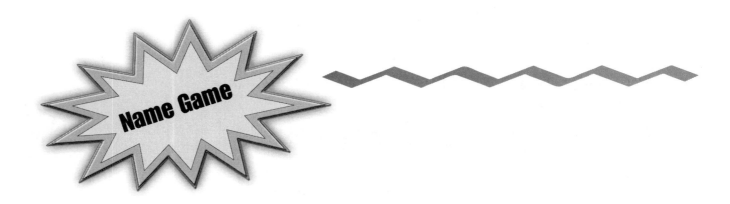

Objective:

Children will be able to classify their classmates' names by the number of syllables.

Materials and Construction:

- 4" x 6" (10 cm x 15.24 cm) unlined index cards (one for each child)
- Marker
- Three empty shoe boxes

Prepare a name tag for each child using a marker and 4" x 6" (10 cm x 15.24 cm) unlined index cards. Use the marker to label three empty shoe boxes with the numbers "1," "2," and "3" (one number per box). If you have children in your class whose names have four or more syllables, label extra shoe boxes with the appropriate numbers ("4," "5," etc.).

Procedures:

Choose one child's name tag and model how to clap the number of syllables in the name. Have children clap the syllables with you. Repeat this procedure with several different names. Ask a child to come up to the front of the group. Show her the three boxes with the numbers on them. Have the child say her name. Ask children to clap the number of syllables in the child's name. Then, have the child place her name tag in the correct shoe box. For example, Tammy would place her name tag in box number 2.

Adaptations:

- Use manila folders instead of shoe boxes. Place a photo of each child on the name tag next to his name. With partners or independently, encourage children to sort the names into the correct folders based on the number of syllables.
- Play the Name Game using children's last names.

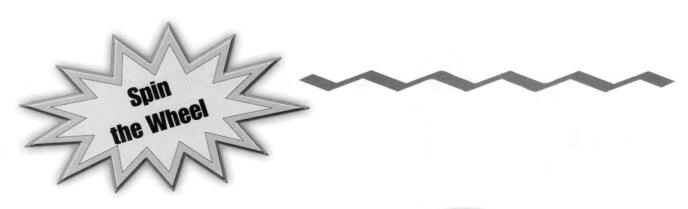

Objective:

Children will be able to classify the number of syllables in environmental print based on the number on a spinner.

Materials and Construction:

- Variety of environmental print (product labels, logos, signs, etc.) with one, two, and three syllables
- A commercial spinner with three sections numbered "1," "2," and "3" or create one using:
  - One sheet of 8.5" x 11" (21.6 cm x 28 cm) card stock
  - One brass fastener
  - Scissors

Cut out environmental print with one, two, and three syllables. Use a spinner from a game that has the numbers 1, 2, and 3. If such a spinner is unavailable, create a spinner by cutting out a circle from the 8.5" x 11" (21.6 cm x 28 cm) card stock. Divide the circle into three equal sections and number the sections "1," "2," and "3." Cut an arrow from card stock and attach it to the center of the circle with a brass fastener.

Procedures:

Introduce this activity to a small group of children. Place the environmental print on a table or the floor so that children can see all of the print. Direct children to name each piece of environmental print. Then, model the activity by spinning the spinner and reading the number. Find a piece of environmental print with the same number of syllables as the number you read. Read the environmental print. Have children take turns following the modeled procedure.

Adaptation:

- Have children complete this activity with partners.

Objective:

Children will be able to tap the number of syllables that they hear when they read environmental print.

Materials and Construction:

- One set of rhythm sticks for each child
- Variety of environmental print (product labels, logos, signs, etc.) with one, two, and three syllables

Procedures:

Display three pieces of environmental print that have different numbers of syllables (one, two, and three) and identify each piece. Select one piece of environmental print, but do not tell the children which piece you have selected. Tell children that you will show them how many syllables are in the environmental print that you selected. Using the rhythm sticks, tap the number of syllables in the environmental print. Ask children to identify which one of the three pieces of environmental print you selected by counting the number of times the sticks tapped. Encourage them to tap the syllables in the same product name with their sticks. Have children say the product name as they tap the syllables.

Adaptations:

- With a small group of children, select an environmental print label/logo from the word wall. Say the name of the product aloud. Direct the children to tap the number of syllables in the product name.
- Have children tap the number of syllables in their names using the rhythm sticks. Then, ask each child to find one piece of environmental print that has the same number of syllables as his name.

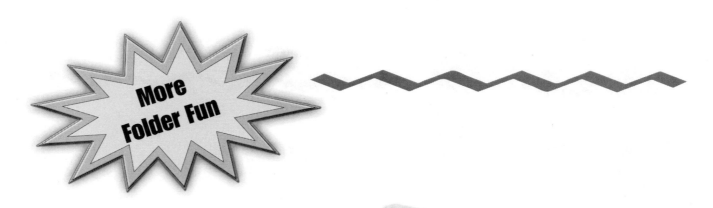

Objective:

Children will be able to classify environmental print by the number of syllables.

Materials and Construction:

- File folder
- Variety of environmental print (product labels, logos, signs, etc.) with one, two, and three syllables
- Marker
- Ruler

Use the marker to divide the file folder into three equal columns. Number the columns "1," "2," "3," from left to right at the top of the columns. Introduce the activity through individualized instruction, then expand it to include small groups.

Procedures:

Ask a child to select a piece of environmental print and clap the number of syllables in the product name. After the child has correctly identified the number of syllables, have her place the environmental print under the correct number in the folder. Continue until each card has been matched to the correct number of syllables.

Adaptations:

- Use only one kind of product label (for example, cereal box fronts).
- Have children complete the activity with partners.

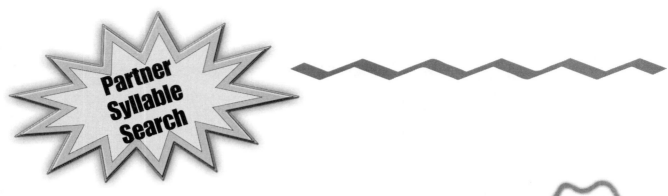

Objective:

Each child will be able to find another child with an environmental print sign that has the same number of syllables as his sign.

Materials and Construction:

- 5" x 8" (12.7 cm x 20.3 cm) unlined index cards
- Variety of environmental print (product labels, logos, signs, etc.) with one, two, and three syllables
- Scissors
- Glue stick
- Hole punch
- Yarn

Cut out environmental print and glue each piece onto a 5" x 8" (12.7 cm x 20.3 cm) unlined index card. Punch holes in the top two corners of each card and tie yarn to the card to make a necklace.

Procedures:

Give each child an environmental print card to wear as a necklace. As a class, clap the number of syllables on each environmental print card. Have children search for partners who have environmental print cards with the same number of syllables as their own cards.

Adaptations:

- Give one child an environmental print card necklace. Ask the child to clap the number of syllables in the environmental print word. Then, have the child select another necklace. Instruct the child to give the new necklace to a classmate who must clap the correct number of syllables in the environmental print. The activity continues until each child in the group has a necklace.
- Have children find partners. Then, have the two partners add the number of syllables in their words. Encourage children to find the highest or lowest total number of syllables.

Incorporate Environmental Print in Centers

The room arrangement in early childhood programs typically has centers in which children can work and play. Often these centers include Blocks, Manipulatives, Art, Music, and Housekeeping. With a little creative thinking and planning, environmental print materials can easily be incorporated into each center area. Surrounding children with print helps them recognize its importance as a means of communication. If teachers begin by incorporating these suggestions, they can enrich each center and provide children with additional opportunities to interact with print in meaningful ways.

Blocks Center

Community Mural

Take photos of buildings in your community (grocery store, post office, fast-food restaurants, etc.). Display the photos on the walls in the Blocks Center or create a mural of the community with the children. Take pictures of street and traffic signs to add to the mural. Point out the names of the buildings as children are working in the Blocks area. Encourage children to create community buildings with the blocks.

Community Blocks

Cut out the names and/or logos of stores, community buildings, fast-food restaurants, etc., from advertisements or products. Glue and shellac the names onto blocks. Encourage children to create buildings from blocks and use the blocks with names and/or logos to complete the buildings.

Traffic and Street Signs

Add traffic and street signs to the Blocks Center. Make sure to include an "Under Construction" sign that children can use if they want to keep working on their buildings later.

Environmental Print Blocks

Make cardboard blocks from empty cereal, cracker, cookie, or Jell-O® boxes. Stuff the boxes with newspaper to make them sturdier. Children can use these blocks for construction projects. Have children sort the blocks by product category.

Drawing and Labeling

Place paper and markers in the Blocks Center. Children can write labels for their buildings. They may also draw pictures of their block constructions and label them.

Manipulatives Center

Jell-O® Patterns

Collect several flavors of empty Jell-O® Gelatin boxes. Stuff the boxes with newspaper to make them sturdy. Use the empty Jell-O® boxes to create patterns. Have children complete the patterns with additional Jell-O® boxes. Other boxed products could also be used to create patterns.

Lacing Cards

Cut the front panels from empty cereal, cookie, or cracker boxes. Use a hole punch to create lacing cards from these front panels. Vary the number of holes to be laced. Attach yarn or shoestrings to the cards for lacing.

Sequencing

Create sequence cards that incorporate environmental print. A morning sequence, for example, could include pictures of a child waking up, dressing for school, eating Apple Jacks®, and going to school.

Milk Jug Cap Sorting

Download images of environmental print from the Internet. Resize the images so that they will fit on milk jug caps. Print the images on sticker paper, cut out, and attach to milk jug caps. If sticker paper is unavailable, print the images on regular paper and glue to the caps. Children can sort the environmental print on the milk jug caps.

What's Missing?

Play "What's Missing?" with children. Create sets of environmental print cards by cutting the front panels from packages or by downloading and printing the images onto 3" x 5" (7.6 cm x 12.7 cm) unlined index cards. These cards could include sets of drinks or snacks. Take one set of products and place the cards on a tray. Ask one child to remove a product while the other children cover their eyes. Then, have the other children guess which product card was removed.

Puzzles

Create puzzles from the front panels of product boxes (see page 10). Vary the number of puzzle pieces based on the skill-level of the children.

Folder Matching Games

Create individual matching games using manila folders. Open the folder and use a marker to divide it into six equal rectangles. Glue the label from a product in each rectangle. The difficulty level will be determined by the products placed in the rectangles. An easy matching game may have a completely different product in each rectangle, such as a drink, a cracker, canned fruit, a candy bar, yogurt, and peanut butter. A more difficult matching game could have a different type of soup can label in each rectangle, such as tomato, chicken noodle, clam chowder, lentil, minestrone, and vegetable. After the folder is complete, create six cards that match the items in the rectangles on the folder. Cover the folder and cards with clear contact paper or laminate for durability. Have children match the item on each card to the same item on the folder. Store the matching games in resealable, plastic bags.

Art Center

Weaving Environmental Print

Find logos that can be cut into 10" x 1" (25 cm x 2.5 cm) strips or glue several smaller logos onto 10" x 1" (25 cm x 2.5 cm) strips of card stock. Use a 10" x 12" (25 cm x 30.5 cm) piece of cardboard to make the loom.

Draw ½" (1.25 cm) vertical lines 1" (2.5 cm) apart across the top and bottom of the cardboard. Using scissors, cut these lines to make notches and tabs. To create the warp, begin by leaving a long piece of yarn hanging at the back of the loom. This may be tied to the end piece of yarn after the warp has been made. Then, wrap yarn around the loom from top to bottom, going into the notches and looping it under the tabs until you have reached the end of the loom (see illustration). Show children how to go over and under the yarn on the loom to weave their environmental print strips.

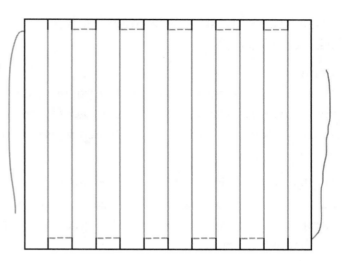

Environmental Print Decoupage

Create a papier-mâché object using balloons, crumpled newspapers, plastic bottles, or aluminum foil as the base. (Keep in mind that uninflated and popped balloons are choking hazards for young children.) Have children use masking tape to keep everything in place as they form the base for the papier-mâché. Then, let children tear newspaper into strips about 1" (2.5 cm) wide. Mix a paste of one part flour and one part water. Show children how to dip the paper strips into the paste and wipe off the excess by holding their fingers in a scissors-like manner. Children should apply the strips to the base in two to three alternating layers, allowing each layer to dry thoroughly. Once the papier-mâché object is complete, attach environmental print that relates to the object with glue. For example, if the papier-mâché object is a cat, use cat food or cat litter labels to cover the cat.

Mobiles

Give children a base from which to hang environmental print. The base and the environmental print hanging from it should be related; for example, a paper bowl base might have cereal logos hanging from it, and a box made to look like a TV could have television show logos hanging from it. Have children attach the environmental print to the base with yarn. The yarn may be taped to the base or threaded through premade holes and tied with your help. Children can work in groups or individually to create the mobiles.

Collage

A collage can be created from a combination of logos, box panels, and flattened plastic bottles glued onto poster or foam board. Cut the board into a shape that represents the theme of the collage. For example, if the board is cut into the shape of a can, children could glue environmental print from canned products on the board. If you cut the board into the shape of a drinking glass, children can create a collage composed of environmental print from beverages such as milk, juice, and Kool-Aid®. Try to use a variety of colors both in the background art and the print.

Neighborhood Mural

If possible, take children on a walking tour of the neighborhood surrounding the school, taking digital pictures along the way. Print these pictures on regular computer paper. You can also cut out pictures of neighborhood stores from newspaper ads. Give children a piece of poster board, a glue stick or watered down glue, and a paintbrush. Have them glue the pictures to the poster board to create a mural of their school's neighborhood.

Pennants
Give each child a piece of construction paper precut to look like a sports pennant. Supply children with sports magazines, sporting goods store advertisements, team logos from the Internet or newspaper, scissors, and a glue stick to complete pennants of their favorite sports teams.

Fine Art
Display fine art prints that incorporate environmental print. Pop art is a great place to begin looking. For example, one of Andy Warhol's *Campbell's Soup Cans* prints could be displayed. Provide a variety of Campbell's® soup labels for children to glue onto finger-paint paper. Then, have children use finger paints to finish their own masterpieces.

Music Center
Making Music
Allow children to make their own musical instruments. To make a maraca, have children fill a large balloon with rice. Then, blow up the balloon and tie a knot in it. (Keep in mind that uninflated and popped balloons are choking hazards for young children.) Children can either crinkle aluminum foil or roll four-inch wide pieces of newspaper to make handles for their maracas. Have children use masking tape to secure the handles to the balloons. Then, let children tear newspaper into strips about 1" (2.5 cm) wide. Next, mix one part flour to one part water to make a papier-mâché paste. Show children how to dip the paper strips into the paste and wipe off the extra paste by holding their fingers in a scissors-like manner. Children should wrap the newspaper strips around the balloon maracas in several layers so the maracas don't break when shaken. Once the papier-mâché has dried, children can glue on environmental print and then shake away.

To make a tambourine, place dry beans between two paper plates and staple them together. Cover the staples with masking tape to cover them, then give children environmental print to glue on their paper plate tambourines.

Bring in cylindrical food containers to use as drums. Oatmeal containers , margarine tubs, and potato chip cans make great drums.

Marching around the Neighborhood
Cut 6" x 6" (15.24 cm x 15.24 cm) squares from card stock. Make enough of these squares so that every child will be able to stand beside one during the activity. Make more squares if desired. Glue local store logos from newspaper advertisements to the squares. Laminate or cover the store cards with clear contact paper or laminate for durability. Introduce each store card to children and have them repeat the names after you. Arrange these store cards in a circle on the floor. Explain to children that you will play music and they should march around the circle of store cards until the music stops. When the music stops, they must stand beside a store card. When the children stop marching, ask several of them what store card they are standing beside. Do this several times until all children have had a chance to participate.

Name That Jingle

Collect environmental print from stores, restaurants, and television shows that have familiar jingles. Glue each piece of environmental print onto a 5" x 8" (12.7 cm x 20.3 cm) unlined index card. Give each child an environmental print card and ask him to read his card to you. Instruct children to hold up their cards when you sing the jingle that goes with their environmental print. For example, the child with a McDonald's® environmental print card would hold it up when you sing the current jingle. As a variation, you can tape record various jingles to play. Have children hold up their cards when the jingles are played on a tape player.

Alphabet Chant

Have children help you create a chant using environmental print. Collect samples of environmental print and glue them onto 5" x 8" (12.7 cm x 20.3 cm) unlined index cards. Pass out one environmental print card to each child. Help children arrange themselves in alphabetical order. Then, the chanting can begin. For example, the A child might say, "A like Apple Jacks®," the B child might say, "B like Burger King®," etc.

Changing the Lyrics

Change the lyrics of favorite children's songs/chants from general words to specific products. For example, you can change the lyrics for the song "Who Stole the Cookies from the Cookie Jar?" to "Who Stole the Oreos® from the Cookie Jar?" Give children product labels that match the product name that will be sung and ask them to hold up their labels when they hear the product name. For example, with "Who Stole the Cookies" several cookie brands could be used so children must listen closely to the song to know when their environmental print will be sung.

Housekeeping Center

Shopping Bags

In addition to having empty food product containers in the housekeeping center, include grocery and other paper shopping bags. Grocery store bags often have the name of the store printed on them and many stores have canvas shopping bags printed with their names and logos. Other shopping bags could come from familiar clothing and department stores. Encourage children to identify the various store logos.

Set the Table

Many restaurants have cups, plates, containers, napkins, and place mats with their names and/or logos printed on them. You can obtain such items from the restaurants for free or for a small charge. Place these items in the Housekeeping Center for children to use. Have children dictate stories about their favorite meals in restaurants.

Cooking

Include food coupons in the housekeeping center. You can make a recipe book or recipe cards by gluing several food coupons on each page or card. Encourage children to copy their favorite recipes to take home to share with their families.

Scrub-a-Dub-Dub

Add empty (and well-rinsed) cleaning supply bottles to the housekeeping area. Some bottles to include are laundry detergent, fabric softener, dish washing liquid, and soap bottles. Encourage children to classify the various products.

Phone Book

Make your own phone book using environmental print. Glue the names and/or logos for restaurants such as Pizza Hut®, McDonald's®, Burger King®, and Dairy Queen® on separate pages. Write the phone numbers (real or made-up) below the environmental print. You can also include neighborhood stores in the phone book. Provide children with opportunities to place food orders or call for store information using the phones in the Housekeeping Center.

Dramatic Play Literacy Centers

Most preschools, early learning, and child care centers have designated various play centers in their classrooms. Adapt your play centers into literacy centers by adding environmental print and other reading and writing materials. This can easily be accomplished by visiting local business establishments and asking for any materials with their logos—bags, containers, sample receipts, hats, coupons, etc. Depending on what you collect, you can create a variety of environmental print literacy centers. Transform your Housekeeping Center into a restaurant, grocery store, post office, hair salon/barbershop, doctor's office, or travel agency by changing the props. By adding menus, rebus recipes, food product containers, signs, and coupons, your Housekeeping Center can become a restaurant. Include a sign with the name of your restaurant, and it is "open for business"! Providing food containers of all shapes and sizes, grocery bags, adding machine paper, and food advertisements creates a grocery store and encourages children to make grocery lists and shop for their favorite foods. Adding postcards, stamps and stampers, envelopes, and stationery makes children feel like they are in the local post office. Providing clean and empty shampoo and conditioner bottles, styling gel containers, and magazines turns the Housekeeping Center into a hair salon/barbershop. Adding travel flyers, samples of airline company logos, vacation brochures, blank credit card receipts, and ticket stubs converts the area into a travel agency and encourages children to plan their dream vacations.

Follow the instructional notes for each dramatic play literacy center and collect as many of the props and suggested books that you can to create these interactive learning areas in your classroom.

Dramatic Play Literacy Center—Grocery Store

Goals

This dramatic play center will enable children to—

1. Read and identify environmental print that they would find in a grocery store
2. Develop their vocabularies by using environmental print

3. Develop cooperative learning skills by playing various roles, such as grocer, shopper, bagger, delicatessen manager, dairy manager, meat manager, etc.
4. Become familiar with various product sections in a grocery store
5. Practice their writing skills for a real purpose by creating grocery lists
6. Classify food labels and logos

Instructional Notes:

Introduce this dramatic play literacy center by showing a bag full of groceries and inviting children to name each product. Ask them to help you classify the groceries by the type of product and then place like products together in a designated area in your new grocery store. Direct children to share personal experiences that they have had while grocery shopping. Ask them if their parents prepare a shopping list before they go to the store and share reasons why they might. Generate a list of local grocery stores and ask them to match grocery bags to the correct grocery stores. Encourage children to name the grocery store workers and show them sample name tags. Explain to children that they will be able to make their own grocery lists and use them to go shopping at this center.

Suggested Props:

- Environmental print
- Variety of empty food containers and boxes, household product containers, frozen food containers, and fruit foam trays
- Name tags for store managers, cashiers, and store department managers
- Signs: Open/Closed; Exit; Hours of Operation; display signs for the various departments, such as Meat Department, Dairy, Frozen Foods, Fruit and Vegetables, etc.
- Scanner, cash register, play money, credit card slips, and ATM machine
- Newspaper grocery advertisements and note pads
- Pens, pencils, and markers
- Coupons
- Plastic and paper bags
- Grocery carts
- Balance scales

Books to Include in This Center:

- *Don't Forget the Bacon!* by Pat Hutchins (HarperTrophy, 1989)
- *Going to the Grocery Store* by Cindy A. Bailey (DRL Books, Inc., 2002)
- *Grocery Store (Field Trip!)* by Angela Leeper (Heinemann, 2004)
- *Jonathan Goes to the Grocery Store* by Susan K. Baggette (Brookfield Reader, 1998)
- *Something Good* by Robert Munsch (Annick Press, 1990)
- *A Visit to the Supermarket* by B. A. Hoena (Pebble Plus, 2004)

Dramatic Play Literacy Center—Restaurant

Goals:

This dramatic play literacy center will enable the children to—

1. Read and identify environmental print that they would find in a restaurant
2. Develop their vocabularies by using environmental print
3. Develop concepts of numbers and counting by using play money
4. Develop menu reading skills by ordering from a menu
5. Develop cooperative learning skills by playing various roles, such as server, manager, customer, cook, cashier, etc.
6. Practice their writing skills for real purposes by writing down customer orders and creating receipts for customers

Instructional Notes:

Introduce this dramatic play literacy center after a discussion about a local restaurant. Set up the center with different props and environmental print to provide a hands-on restaurant experience. Gather as many real-life props as you can. Invite children to act out different roles (server, manager, customer, etc.) to make this center meaningful.

Suggested Props:

- Environmental print
- Name tags for chef and service staff
- Menus
- Bills/checks
- Signs: Open/Closed, No Smoking, Exit, Hours of Operation
- Coupons
- Menus and daily specials
- Rebus recipes
- Labels
- Reservation book
- Suggestion box
- Table settings (plates, cups, silverware, etc.)
- Food products (empty containers)
- Cash register, play money, and receipts
- Chef's hats and aprons
- Table and chairs
- Order pads, pens, pencils, and markers

Books to Include in this Center:

- *Dinner at the Panda Palace* by Stephanie Calmenson (HarperTrophy, 1995)
- *Friday Night at Hodges' Cafe* by Tim Egan (Houghton Mifflin, 1996)

- *Froggy Eats Out* by Jonathan London (Puffin Books, 2003)
- *Little Nino's Pizzeria* by Karen Barbour (Voyager Books, 1990)
- *Miss Piggy's Night Out* by Sara Hoagland Hunter (Viking Children's Books, 1995)
- *The Moon & Riddles Diner and the Sunnyside Café* by Nancy Willard (Harcourt Children's Books, 2001)
- *Pollen Pie* by Louise Argiroff (Atheneum Books, 1988)

Dramatic Play Literacy Center—Hair Salon/Barbershop

Goals:
This dramatic play center will enable the children to—

1. Read and identify environmental print that they would find in a hair salon/barbershop
2. Develop their vocabularies by using environmental print
3. Develop cooperative learning skills by playing various roles, such as hairstylist, customer, cashier, manager, etc.
4. Develop concepts of numbers and counting by pricing various hair product containers and by using play money
5. Practice writing for a real purpose by dictating a story about a trip to the hair salon/barbershop
6. Classify a variety of hair-related environmental print by category

Instructional Notes:
Introduce this dramatic play literacy center after someone in the class gets a haircut and after a discussion about a local hair salon/barbershop. Set up the center with props and environmental print to provide a hands-on hair salon/barbershop experience. Gather as many real life props as you can. Invite parents to help you stock this center with empty product containers from home. Encourage children to take turns acting out the various roles.

Suggested Props:
- Environmental print
- Name tags for hairstylist, manicurist, barber, shop owner, and manager
- Signs: Open/Closed, No Smoking, Exit, Hours of Operation, Cost of Services (haircuts, shampoos, perms, shaves, color treatments, manicures, and pedicures)
- Appointment book and appointment cards
- Variety of empty bottles and containers for hair products (shampoo and conditioner, hair spray, styling gel, and mousse) nail polish and remover, and shaving-cream
- Cash register, play money, and receipts
- Telephone and note pads
- Large shirts or smocks for cover-ups

- Chairs, cordless hair dryers and curling irons, hair rollers, combs, brushes and hair picks, bobby pins and barrettes, bladeless plastic razors
- Used, popular hairstyle magazines

Books to Include in This Center:
- *Aaron's Hair* by Robert Munsch (Cartwheel, 2002)
- *Makeup Mess* by Robert Munsch (Cartwheel, 2002)
- *Stephanie's Ponytail* by Robert Munsch (Annick Press, 1996)

Dramatic Play Literacy Center—Travel Agency

Goals:
This dramatic play center will enable the children to—

1. Read and identify environmental print that one would find in a travel agency
2. Develop their vocabularies by using environmental print
3. Develop cooperative learning skills by playing various roles, such as travel agent, business manager, ticket agent, tourist, flight attendant, train conductor, tour guide, etc.
4. Become familiar with a variety of places that are popular to visit
5. Practice their writing skills for a real purpose by creating postcards of places to visit
6. Become familiar with using maps and globes to locate particular tourist spots
7. Classify travel-related environmental print

Instructional Notes:
Introduce this dramatic play literacy center at the beginning of the school year. Ask children if they traveled anywhere over the summer. Show them a large map and a globe and pinpoint the places that are mentioned. Ask them what they did on their vacations that was fun and record their answers on chart paper. Tell them that an adult can earn a living by planning vacation trips for people who want to travel. Show them various travel brochures, airplane and train tickets, and travel route maps or other props that you have collected. Invite the parents to provide travel memorabilia. Explain the various roles that the children can play in this center.

Suggested Props:
- Environmental print
- Name tags for travel agents, baggage handlers, tour guides, and tourists
- Samples of bus, train, and airplane tickets, airline magazines, air-sickness bags, empty pretzel bags, flight plans
- Travel brochures, large travel posters, travel agendas, travel schedules, luggage tags, and postcards
- Signs: Open/Closed, Flight Schedule displays, Reservations sheets
- Cash register, play money, and credit card slips

- Telephone and note pads
- Globes and maps
- Chairs
- Table to use as a counter

Books to Include in This Center:
- *Angela's Airplane* by Robert Munsch (Annick Press, 1988)
- *Freight Train* by Donald Crews (Greenwillow, 1996)
- *Hey! Get Off Our Train* by John Burningham (Dragonfly Books, 1994)
- *Shortcut* by Donald Crews (HarperTrophy, 1996)
- *Space Travel* by S. Attmore (Brimax Books, 1985)
- *Thomas the Tank Engine* by The Reverend W. Awdry (Random House Books for Young Children, 2005)

Dramatic Play Literacy Center—Post Office

Goals:
This dramatic play literacy center will enable the children to—

1. Read and identify environmental print that they would find in a post office
2. Develop their vocabularies by using environmental print
3. Develop basic skills of letter writing (heading, body, closing)
4. Develop concept of numbers and counting using play money
5. Create their own letterheads, postcards, stamps, and address labels using environmental print
6. Classify environmental print by TV-show, store, or restaurant names

Instructional Notes:
Set up this dramatic play literacy center after taking children to the local post office or reading a book such as *The Post Office Book: Mail and How It Moves* by Gail Gibbons (HarperTrophy, 1986) or *To the Post Office with Mama* by Sue Farrell (Annick Press, 1994). When assembling supplies for this center, gather as many real-life props as possible. Encourage parents to help you stock your post office with paper and envelopes that have company logos and letterheads, if possible.

Have children make materials to be included in the center. Allow children to make their own letterheads using environmental print letters to spell their names, then make additional copies for them to use in the center. Give children magazines so that they can use pictures of places to make postcards using large index cards. Allow children to write letters to their classmates. The letters can be dropped into a "mailbox," sorted, and delivered when the post office is open. Invite children to take turns being the mail carrier and postmaster. Remind them to pick up their mail before they leave each day. Once children become familiar with writing letters and addressing envelopes, encourage them to write to friends in other classes or to their parents or other relatives.

Suggested Props:

- Environmental print
- Signs: Post Office, Open/Closed, Post Office Hours, Exit
- Displays for Overnight Express, Special Delivery, Collectable Stamps, etc.
- Mailbox made from a large cardboard box
- Individual mailboxes/post office boxes (can be made from cereal boxes stacked together)
- Name tags for postmaster, postal workers, and mail carrier
- Names of classmates to be used when writing letters
- Logos from favorite TV shows, stores, and restaurants to use for address/return address labels
- Table for writing letters
- Table to use as a counter
- Plain and letterhead paper
- Envelopes
- Blank cards and postcards
- Index cards and old magazines for postcards
- Old, return address labels
- Postmarked/cancelled stamps
- Stampers that can be used to stamp envelopes
- Pens, pencils, and markers
- Glue sticks
- Cash register and play money
- Scale to weigh packages and letters
- Duffle bag or gym bag to use as a mailbag

Books to Include in This Center:

- *Birthday Card, Where Are You?* by Harriet Ziefert (Viking Children's Books, 1985)
- *Mr. Griggs' Work* by Cynthia Rylant (Scholastic, 1993)
- *Penguin Post* by Debi Gliori (Harcourt Children's Books, 2002)
- *The Post Office Book: Mail and How It Moves* by Gail Gibbons (HarperTrophy, 1986)
- *To the Post Office with Mama* by Sue Farrell (Annick Press, 1994)
- *Will Goes to the Post Office* by Olof and Lena Landström (R & S Books, 2001)

Dramatic Play Literacy Center—Doctor's Office

Goals:
This dramatic play literacy center will enable the children to—

1. Read and identify environmental print that they would find in a doctor's office
2. Develop their vocabularies by using environmental print
3. Develop cooperative learning skills by role-playing various roles, such as doctor, nurse, receptionist, physician's assistant, patient, etc.

4. Develop nonstereotypical concepts of gender roles in the work force
5. Develop concepts of numbers and counting by using play money and scale

Instructional Notes:

This center should be introduced after discussing children's experiences with their own doctors. Point out that doctors and nurses can be men or women. While introducing the medicine bottles, stress the importance of never taking any real medicine unless it is given to them by a trusted adult. Supply as many real-life props as possible for this center. Doctors' offices and hospitals may be willing to donate items. Pharmacies may provide empty, new medicine bottles.

Suggested Props:

- Signs: Open/Closed, Exit, Exam Room 1, Name of Doctor's Office (for example, Feel Better Pediatrics)
- Sign-in book
- Old magazines for waiting room area
- Realistic doctor kits
- Empty adhesive bandage boxes (Band-Aid®, Curad®, etc.)
- Empty medicine bottles
- Elastic bandages (Ace®, Futuro®, etc.) and boxes
- Eye chart
- Bathroom scale
- Surgical masks
- Surgical gowns
- Surgical slippers
- Realistic prescription pads
- Name tags for doctors and nurses
- Rebus symptom checklist
- Office visit billing statements
- Environmental print insurance cards, featuring logos and names of real insurance companies
- Play money, checks, and money tray

Books to Include in This Center:

- *The Berenstain Bears Go to the Doctor* by Stan and Jan Berenstain (Random House Books for Young Readers, 1981)
- *Corduroy Goes to the Doctor* by Don Freeman (Viking Juvenile, 2005)
- *A Day in the Life of a Doctor* by Linda Hayward (DK Publishing, 2001)
- *Doctor Maisy* by Lucy Cousins (Candlewick Press, 2001)
- *Doctor Tools* by Inez Snyder (Children's Press, 2002)
- *Froggy Goes to the Doctor* by Jonathan London (Puffin Books, 2004)

Word Wall

Teachers call the place in their rooms where they display words a word wall (Cunningham, 2004). A word wall that is developmentally appropriate for young children can easily be created to display environmental print. Build a word wall in your classroom by dividing an area into 26 spaces and placing cards with both uppercase and lowercase forms of each letter in alphabetical order. Allow enough room under each letter for logos or other examples of environmental print to be posted. Begin your word wall by placing cards with the children's names under the matching initial letter. If possible, include photos of the children next to their names. This will get the children's attention and personalize the word wall. Then, gradually add cereal box tops, food packages, and labels under the appropriate letters. Introduce five items a week and encourage children to bring in new logos to add to the word wall.

Make the word wall interactive by putting magnetic strips or hook-and-loop tape on each example of environmental print so that the children can actually take the pictures and word cards down to use.

A Dozen Other Ways to Use a Word Wall

1. Chant the names of the items on the wall. This can be completed in a variety of ways. For example, on Monday the children could find the letter on the word wall that **Monday** starts with (**M**) and chant all of the items on the wall that begin with that letter. Or children could chant all of the words that begin with the same sound as the date, such as **N** for **November**, or **T** for the **tenth** day of the month. This activity could also be tied to birthdays or special events.

2. Play "I Spy" by saying, "I spy something that says 'Snap! Crackle! Pop!®'" (Rice Krispies®) or "I spy something to eat for breakfast that begins with **C**" (Corn Flakes®).

3. Lead children on a scavenger hunt by having each child work with a partner to find the pictures on the word wall that match a preprinted list of products. For example, create a list of different beverages and have children find the matching Kool-Aid®, juice, or soft drink environmental print.

4. Read some of the words/labels every day. Pick a designated time of day to review the words on the environmental print wall by reading them aloud with the whole group. You may choose to review words that begin with a certain letter of a child's name or choose to review a whole section of the wall. For example, after the morning meeting would be an ideal time to ask the children to read all of the environmental print that begins with the same letter sound as "Billy." The goal is to make environmental print part of the daily routine so that the children become accustomed to using the words and logos.

5. Conduct a speed drill. Direct children to locate specific items as fast as they can. Choose two children and give each of them a pointer. Call out a label or a word and ask the children to locate and point to that item as quickly as they can. Have the rest of the class read the name of the correct item together and then select another pair of children to repeat the same procedure.

6. Hold up a letter card and ask children to name the environmental print on the wall that begins with that letter. Select a letter with which the class has been working. You could also select a letter that begins two or more children's names in your class. Then, direct children to name the environmental print on the wall that begins with that letter.

7. Play "I'm Lost" by taking down a few items from the word wall and asking volunteers to find their spots on the wall and place them back where they belong.

8. Play "Let's Go Shopping" by encouraging children to use the products on the wall to make shopping lists of items that they could buy at a grocery store, speciality store, or toy store.

9. Remove some items from the wall and challenge the children to sort them into categories. If a variety of cereal box fronts or box tops are displayed on the wall, use them with a variety of other products and ask children to group all of the cereals together.

10. Photocopy some of the objects from the word wall and send them home so that children can share them with their families.

11. Build on children's awareness of numbers by counting the objects under each letter. Use terms like **most** and **fewest** to describe the quantity.

12. Help develop children's rhyming skills by pointing to a product name on the word wall and encouraging them to find a word that rhymes with it. For example, "For breakfast, I like to eat Trix®. My mom likes to eat _____ (Kix®)."

After you have an environmental print word wall growing in your room, you will be delighted to see how frequently the children use it in their daily activities. It can serve as a springboard to build literacy skills and reinforce the skills from the Environmental Print Learning Continuum.

Parents as Partners

Involving parents in their children's education is a primary goal for all preschool programs. To achieve this goal, it is imperative to inform parents about environmental print. In this section of the book, there is a letter (page 92) that explains what environmental print is and describes ways that parents can help their children identify environmental print. This letter also invites parents to collect environmental print samples and encourages them to send these to school with their child. There is space at the top and bottom of the letter for you to attach examples of environmental print before making copies.

There is also a letter to parents (page 93) that asks them to respond to a survey about their child's awareness of environmental print. This survey should be sent out twice, once after you have sent home the explanation letter, and then a month later after you have begun using the activities for each step of the continuum. The parents should be able to see a big difference in their child's ability to read and recognize environmental print!

Other Ways to Encourage Family Involvement

After you have informed parents about environmental print and have collected the survey responses, you will be ready to involve the parents in other ways. Suggested activities that families can be part of include:

1. Sponsor an "Environmental Print Games Night." Set up stations around the room for children and their parents to play the following games from the Environmental Print Activities section: Vegetable Concentration (see page 17), Neighborhood Egg Match (see page 18), and Traffic Symbol Bingo (see page 24).

2. Send home an invitation for families to go on a "Community Word Hunt." Encourage children and their families go on a neighborhood scavenger hunt to find:
   - 5 traffic signs
   - 4 names of local businesses
   - 3 names of fast food places
   - 2 food products
   - 1 toy advertisement

   Families can either draw the signs or take pictures of them to share in school.

3. Encourage families to clip and match coupons from newspapers or magazines to play Environmental Print Concentration.

4. Suggest that families make books of their favorite cereals, candies, etc., by gluing the actual box or wrapper on paper, stapling the papers together, and reading the book aloud as a "bedtime story."

5. Encourage families to buy Alpha-Bits® cereal, pasta, or pretzels shaped like letters of the alphabet so that children can spell out their favorite products.

6. Ask parents to help their children construct environmental print bags by putting product labels and logos that they have been collecting into gift bags or any bag with handles. Each child should write her name on the front of the bag and add a logo or other example of environmental print. Children should then practice reading the environmental print with their parents and bring the bags to school to share with their classmates.

Dear Parents,

Environmental print is a term that all parents of every young reader should know. It is the print that we see all around us: the labels on cookies and cereal that your child loves, the logo of a favorite fast-food restaurant, and the stop sign at the corner. It is the print that we recognize from the colors, pictures, and shapes that surround us.

Environmental print is usually the first print that children recognize. They gradually begin to read the words, first without the color and then without the pictures and shapes that surround them. Recognizing environmental print makes children feel successful at reading and motivates them to read more.

You can encourage your child to read environmental print. All day long, there are opportunities to point out print to your child. As you prepare meals, read the labels of food items. When you run errands or are driving in the car, read the traffic signs and billboards. When you walk into a place of business, read signs and the labels of products being sold.

Help me bring environmental print into the classroom. Please begin collecting familiar print samples with your child. Newspaper and magazine ads are an excellent source for print samples, as well as coupons and labels on packaged food. Send in as many coupons, labels, and other print samples as you can. We will use these samples for various activities, including puzzles, educational games, books, and a class scrapbook.

Please start collecting today! Your child will be proud to show classmates how well he or she can read. As always, thank you for helping our young readers grow.

Sincerely,

Dear Parents,

An exciting event in a child's life is learning to read. It happens in many ways, and there are many steps along the road. We're partners in helping your child become a reader. The reading of signs and labels is an exciting stage as your child grows as a reader. I invite you to help me watch for and celebrate the milestones along your child's path to literacy.

Circle the responses below that most closely match what you see your child doing. Then, return the completed survey to me in about a week. I will send the survey home again in about one month so that we can continue to monitor your child's growth in these skills. Please add any other observations you wish to share on the back of the survey.

Thanks!

Child's Name_____ Date _____

1. My child tries to read traffic signs (stop, school crossing, etc.)

    often   occasionally   not yet

2. My child tries to read signs on restaurants and stores (McDonald's®, Sears®, etc.)

    often   occasionally   not yet

3. My child tries to read the text on cereal boxes.

    often   occasionally   not yet

4. My child tries to read the labels on video tapes/DVDs

    often   occasionally   not yet

5. My child tries to read other labels (Coke®, Pepsi®, Milky Way®, Hershey's®, etc.)

    often   occasionally   not yet

Class Checklist for Environmental Print (E. P.)

Directions: Place a check (✓) in the box if the child has demonstrated that skill and can do it independently. Place a plus (+) if the child can do the activity with help. Place a minus (–) in the box if the child cannot perform the skill at this time. Record the number of logos that the child can classify by beginning sound.

Name	Date	Point to E. P.	Match E. P. L=logos W=words	Identify E. P. L=logos S=signs P=product labels	Name Individual Letters in E. P.	Name Copy Decontextualized Word to E. P.	Match Classify E. P. by Category	Dictate a Story Using E. P.	Classify E. P. by Beginning Sound	Classify E. P. by Number of Syllables

Student Checklist for Environmental Print

Student's Name _____ Age_____ Date _____

Recorder _____

1. Can **point** to environmental print

    ___Yes   ___No   ___With help

2. Can **identify** environmental print

    ___Yes   ___No   ___With help

3. Can **match** environmental print

    ___Yes   ___No   ___With help

4. Can **name** individual letters in environmental print

    ___Yes   ___No   ___With help

5. Can **copy** environmental print

    ___Yes   ___No   ___With help

6. Can **match** decontextualized text to environmental print

    ___Yes   ___No   ___With help

7. Can **classify** environmental print by category

    ___Yes   ___No   ___With help

8. Can **dictate** a story using environmental print

    ___Yes   ___No   ___With help

9. Can **classify** environmental print by initial sound

    ___0-4 pieces of environmental print by beginning sound

    ___5-9 pieces of environmental print by beginning sound

    ___10 or more pieces of environmental print by beginning sound

10. Can **classify** environmental print by initial sound

    ___0-4 pieces of environmental print by _____ syllables

    ___5-9 pieces of environmental print by _____ syllables

    ___10 or more pieces of environmental print by _____ syllables

Comments:

Professional References

Armbruster, B. B., F. Lehr, and J. Osborn. 2001. *Put reading first: The research building blocks for teaching children to read*. Washington, DC: Partnership for Reading. http://www.nifl.gov/partnershipfor-reading/publications/reading_first1.html (accessed May 24, 2004)

Beaty, J. J. and Pratt, L. 2002. *Early literacy in preschool and kindergarten*. Upper Saddle River, NJ.: Prentice Hall.

Beeler, T. 1993. *I can read! I can write! Creating a print-rich environment*. Huntington Beach, CA: Creative Teaching Press.

Cunningham, P. M. 2004. *Phonics they use: Words for reading and writing. (4th ed.)*. New York: Allyn & Bacon.

Fields, M. V., K. L. Spangler, and L. Groth. 2003. *Let's begin reading right*. Upper Saddle River, NJ: Prentice Hall.

Harste, J., C. L. Burke, and V. A. Woodward. 1982. Children, their language and world: Initial encounters with print. In *Reader meets author: Bridging the gap*, ed. J. A. Langer and M. T. Smith-Burke, 105–131. Newark, DE: International Reading Association.

Morrow, L. M. 2004. *Literacy development in the early years: Helping children read and write*. Boston, MA: Allyn & Bacon.

Morrow, L. M., D. S. Strickland, and D. G. Woo. 1998. *Literacy instruction in half and whole-day kindergarten: Research to practice*. Newark, DE: International Reading Association.

Owocki, G. 2001. *Make way for literacy: Teaching the way young children learn*. Portsmouth, NH: Heinemann.

Tompkins, G. E. 2002. *Literacy for the 21st century: Teaching reading and writing in pre-kindergarten through grade 4*. Upper Saddle River, NJ.: Prentice Hall.

West, L. S. and E. H. Egley. 1998. Children get more than a hamburger: Using labels and logos to enhance literacy. *Dimensions of Early Childhood* 26 (3/4): 43–46.